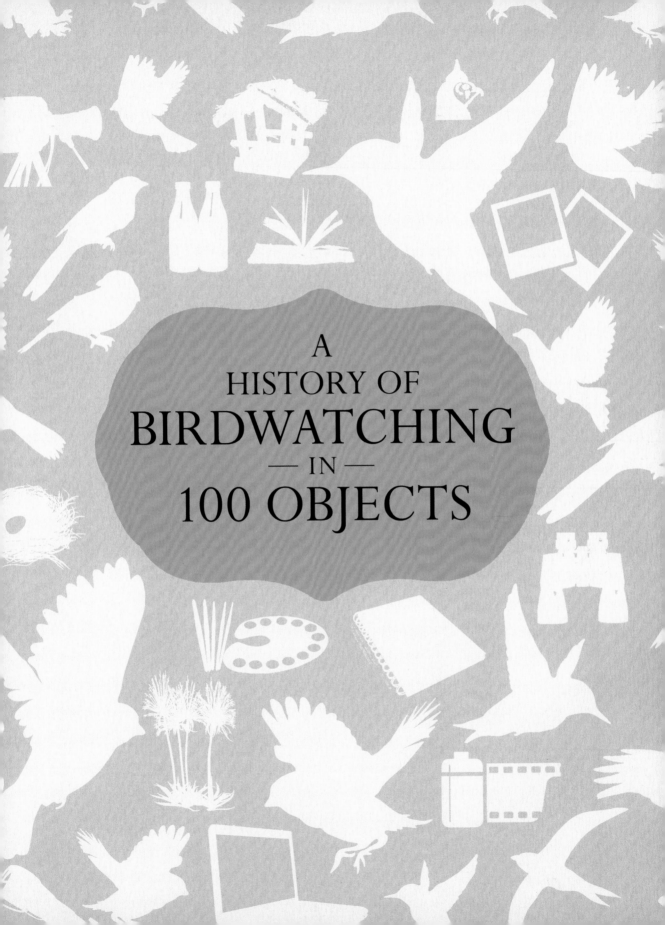

A HISTORY OF
BIRDWATCHING
— IN —
100 OBJECTS

A
HISTORY OF
BIRDWATCHING
— IN —
100 OBJECTS

DAVID CALLAHAN

EDITED BY DOMINIC MITCHELL

BLOOMSBURY

LONDON • NEW DELHI • NEW YORK • SYDNEY

Published 2014 by Bloomsbury Publishing Plc,
50 Bedford Square, London WC1B 3DP

www.bloomsbury.com

Bloomsbury is a trademark of Bloomsbury Publishing Plc

ISBN (print) 978-1408-1-8618-3
ISBN (epub) 978-1408-1-8666-4
ISBN (epdf) 978-1408-1-8665-7

A CIP catalogue record for this book is available from the British Library

This book is produced using paper that is made from wood grown
in managed sustainable forests. It is natural, renewable and
recyclable. The logging and manufacturing processes conform
to the environmental regulations of the country of origin.

Design: Nicola Liddiard, Nimbus Design

Printed in China by C & C Offset Printing Co Ltd

10 9 8 7 6 5 4 3 2 1

Editor's foreword

Much has been written about the history of birdwatching, from its early pioneers and famous sons to its centuries-long development and convoluted social history. Once the territory of explorers and colonels and the pastime of clergymen and Edwardian ladies, it now has a large army of devotees at all levels, from garden birdwatchers and keen local 'patchers' to conservation fieldworkers and globe-trotting listers.

In the modern birding era, people from many different backgrounds, sometimes with little else in common, find themselves united by a shared interest in birds. For the keenest, it is integral to who they are, not just what they do. And the origins of their obsession can often be traced back not only by the conventional historical process, but also through critical events and objects which have had a profound and lasting impact.

I first mused over a selection of historically 'defining' birding items back in 2010. My initial thoughts were improved through editorial discussion and debate at *Birdwatch* magazine, after which the idea came to life as a series of 25 objects through the authorship of David Callahan. Most were obvious choices, a few were more controversial, but all were significant in some way in the development of birdwatching.

Here, in a new and more expansive format, that selection has been refined, developed and extended to 100 objects. While it's tempting to describe it as definitive, the reality is that there can be no absolute list. Many readers may find themselves in agreement with most of the items but not all, an inevitable outcome when the choices also reflect personal opinion, interpretation and individual significance. Whatever the shortlist, it has been an intriguing perspective to take on the history of this most absorbing of interests.

Dominic Mitchell

CONTENTS

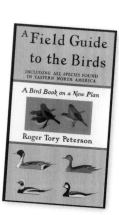

Introduction

The practice of birdwatching – or birding to use its more modern handle – is a sensory occupation at its most basic; it entails using and exercising natural visual and aural capabilities to their very limits, to observe the appearance and activities of birds in the wild.

But human limitations become apparent very quickly even when you're 'in the zone', and it is obvious that some sort of aid will be needed to get you closer to the animal in question, to record its physical characteristics and sounds, and the time and place that you saw it.

To these ends humans have employed methods both simple and complex, and it is these technological advances that have driven the hobby almost from its very beginnings as observations of bird behaviour by hunters and farmers, often essential to their survival. This book aims to chronologically compile the essential innovations that have built the hobby into the gadget-heavy popular pastime we know today.

From the first daubings of megafaunal fowl that humans left on cave walls to the digital images we now text, email and post to our blogs, and from the first imitative whistle to the compressed blastings of an iPod in the field, birding has often been as much about the advantages given by its contemporary tools as it has the objects of our fascination.

If you find you're getting 'fear of the gear' a little, then take heart. Despite all the gadgetry and paraphernalia, birding is a hobby in which you can start from scratch and teach yourself. The birds themselves have changed relatively little in the time span of the hobby – you really can still just throw binoculars and a book in a bag, and go birding.

David Callahan

1 : Arnhemland rock painting

c. 45,000 BP

Representations of birds date back as far as the cave and rock paintings of the Paleolithic period, which ended with the retreat of Ice Age glaciation about 10,000 years before present (BP). The oldest known rock art in the world, discovered in south-west Arnhemland in Australia's Northern Territory, depicts two Emu-like ratites daubed in red ochre and is dated at around 45,000 years BP.

The drawings in the ornithological graffiti closely resemble *Genyornis newtoni*, a large, short-legged and stubby-beaked carnivorous ratite resembling the modern-day Emu, believed to have become extinct at around that date, coinciding with the original colonisation of humans – it was possibly even the first anthropogenic extinction.

An alternative theory is that the paintings are younger – the oldest radiocarbon-dated cave drawings being 28,000 years old and from the same region – and provide evidence that *Genyornis* or a similar form became extinct much later than fossils show, probably as a result of the Ice Age. Yet a further possibility is that the painting represents a kind of folk memory of such species, preserved in the local tribes' Jawoyn Dreaming beliefs and drawn as a mythological caricature. If the painting is *Genyornis*, then the rock art represents the first recorded identification of a known species and suggests that throughout the evolution of *Homo sapiens*, birds have played an important cultural role, literally and possibly even spiritually.

Other ancient artistic depictions of birds include an unidentifiable waterfowl in carved mammoth ivory from Hohle Fels Cave, Bavaria, Germany, dated at between 31,000-33,000 years BP; a Carrion Crow head in the lower caves at Grotte d'Oxocelhaya, Pyrénées-Atlantique, France, dated at about 14,000 years BP; and recognisable Sooty Terns drawn about 3,000 years ago on Rapa Nui, Easter Island, in the South Pacific. In fact, as humans spread out of Africa and across the globe, their cave and wall art went with them, and so did their figurative drawings of birds. Africa's cave paintings date back almost 25,000 years, those of India and Asia 12,000 years, and basic 'stick' birds are present on cave walls at Rio Pinturas, Argentina, dated at 9,000 years old.

Many archaeologists have attempted to work out what such illustrations represented psychologically or practically, and there may have been artistic licence and abstract meaning to some; others may represent religious beliefs.

Henri Breuil's idea that these paintings were 'hunting magic' is widely accepted, with hunters believing that the art served to increase the numbers of prey or prevent bad luck; studies of modern hunter-gatherer societies indicate that shamen paint images of wildlife seen in trances to enhance their own 'powers' or represent the will of the gods. In different cultures around the world, cave and

This red ochre rock art painting is thought to represent two flightless
Genyornis newtoni, which probably became extinct about 45,000 years
ago, possibly co-existing with aboriginal Australians for several
thousand years until the Ice Age climate wiped them out.

rock paintings vary from mere lines and hand prints to well-coloured and sophisticated works; hand prints also indicate that they may have been executed by both sexes.

Many bear a more literal and educational interpretation. Much of this ancient artwork may have been created by hunters attempting to pass on seasonal, behavioural and tracking information to each other or to less experienced colleagues, almost as if the walls were a school textbook or a newspaper. This may explain the presence of animal and bird tracks drawn on the walls of some sites, and might also justify the curious aspects of some, portraying animals twisted up at unnatural angles from their tracks, as if graphically illustrating their owner.

Though popularly known for hunting the striking megafauna of the Pleistocene, we can be sure that humans in the distant past more often relied on smaller game, and bird identification and knowledge of their habits would have been paramount when larger animals and seasonal vegetables were unavailable. Intimate observations of the natural world are essential to hunters to this day, and these involve classifying the world around them. Jared Diamond found, in an oft-quoted short paper, that the primitive Fore people of the New Guinean highlands were able to identify 110 taxa, nearly all of which corresponded to species or species complexes recognised by modern science (the remainder were the dimorphic sexes of four bowerbirds and birds-of-paradise).

Such well-observed (though somewhat unempirical) and traditional knowledge would reach a first flowering when the early civilisations of the Middle East, particularly ancient Egypt, evolved and developed agriculture and intensive labour, and consequently the leisure time to begin attempting true 'art for art's sake'. And observation for observation's sake.

2 : The geese of Meidum

c.4,600 BP

The first recorded birds that could clearly be identified to species level by accurately drawn details of their plumage were made by the tomb artists of ancient Egypt, and some of the most eye-catching of these to the modern observer are probably the geese of Meidum, preserved on a tomb decoration panel in the Egyptian Museum, Cairo.

This panel shows six geese, all assignable to three species: Red-breasted Goose, White-fronted Goose and what is either Greylag or possibly Taiga Bean Goose, to judge by size, colour and bill shape. None of these currently winters in Egypt, though the last two species have been recorded as vagrants in the Nile Delta.

The wall painting dates from around 4,600 BP, and was located in a passage in the mud-brick tomb of Itet, wife of Nefermaat, vizier, royal seal bearer, prophet and eldest son of Pharoah Sneferu. It was painted with pigments derived from limestone, iron ore and malachite mixed with egg white, and depicts an autumnal scene once common in daily life along the Nile: northern Palearctic geese feeding on the grasses growing in profusion over the river's huge floodplain.

So far, more than 75 bird species have been identified in the wall art of ancient Egypt, as well as almost 50 species as mummified remains. However, birds meant substantially more to the Egyptians than beautifully rendered pictures, and through the amazing expansion of this over-achieving civilisation, birds entered the written language as 'letters' and 'words', and were viewed as earthly representatives of a god and treated in death as metaphysically equal to humans.

The god Horus was illustrated as having a falcon's head and enfolded the pharoah in its wings in many painted murals, and Sacred Ibis was worshipped as a god and deemed as a suitable sacrifice for Thoth (himself often depicted as a man with the head of an ibis). The deity Thoth represented either the heart and tongue of their ultimate god Ra, or a god in his own right, the creator of science, philosophy, religion and magic, then viewed as facets of the same subject. The Greeks held onto Thoth as the originator of these strands of human endeavour, adding mathematics and language to his talents.

Consequently, Sacred Ibises were killed in their millions and are commonly found as mummies in Egyptian tombs. The purpose of mummification was often to preserve internal organs in the belief that they would continue to

The Meidum wall panel clearly depicts Red-breasted (left) and
probably Greylag Goose, which would probably have wintered
in the region at the time the artwork was created.

function in the afterlife. To this end, ibis
gizzards were removed, embalmed and then
placed back in the visceral cavity, still
containing snail shells from the bird's last
meal; their whole body cavities were then
stuffed with grain.

Egyptian hieroglyphs themselves are the
second oldest major form of written language
after Sumerian cuneiform, and are an
intriguing contextual mix of consonants and
whole words. Representations of ibises
(representing the sound 'gm' and also meaning
to find or discover) also became part of the
writing on tomb walls as hieroglyphics, along
with several other basic bird forms: owl (the
letter 'm'); quail chick (the letter 'w' or 'u', also
indicating plurality); swallow (the sound 'wr',
also meaning 'great'); sparrow ('small' or
'bad'); and vulture (the vowel 'a'). Parts of
birds were also used: the heads of Pintail, an
unknown crested bird (perhaps a Hoopoe),
Spoonbill and vulture, as well as wing feather,
claws and egg.

A hieroglyphic combination of heron and
the fabled phoenix was the mythical being
Bennu, associated with resurrection and the
seasonal rising of the Nile, and with the heart
and soul of Ra himself; counter-intuitively,
this was also illustrated as a Yellow Wagtail or
eagle. A giant species of Middle Eastern heron
is known to have become extinct within the last
5,000 years and may have inspired Bennu
— *Ardea bennuides* grew to over two metres in
height, had a wingspan of up to 2.7m (and a
nest that measured 15m across), dwarfing
Goliath Heron *A. goliath*, a sub-Saharan
African species occasionally seen in Egypt.

Like the birds themselves, Egyptian bird-
myths and pictorial uses are magical and
dramatic, but such a prevalent cultural and
spiritual application also shows how much
birds meant to their complex world view. Birds
would have provided food and were
agricultural pests, as well as being prominent
parts of the local scenery, inspiring artistic
interpretation and inviting explanations of
their meaning, form and behaviour.

It seems our very language and modes of
communication have their origin partly in
observations and representations of birds.

3 : Papyrus bird painting

c. 3,300 BP

Ancient Egyptian depictions of birds did not remain on the rock face but moved to the tomb wall, and commonly appeared on papyri, a material similar to modern paper, and used in much the same way for drawing, painting and writing.

True papyrus is made from the stems of the shallow water sedge *Cyperus papyrus*, which grows at the edge of rivers and lakes, and began being manufactured in the Nile Valley about 5,000 years ago. The plant grows rapidly and extensively, and formed harvestable swamps on the Nile's floodplain, its use enabling an explosion of written and illustrated communication during the growth of ancient Egyptian civilisation. In fact, much of Egyptian society also relied upon the rich biota of the papyrus stands, which provided birds and mammals for hunting, and formed breeding grounds for a profusion of edible fish; the Nile itself deposited the highly productive soils of the region. It is thought that the later decline of the Egyptian Empire could be indirectly attributed to over-exploitation of these fecund resources.

The papyrus sedge also represents the retreat of a particular habitat back into the 'Dark Continent'. The plants are relied upon by several species of heron, warbler and weaver, many of which are still found in Egypt, but in different proportions as the specialist habitat is now very scarce. It is likely that more southern African species may have lived to the north of their current range in Egypt when the swamps were at their full extent.

Gradually, the Nile was changed by the conflicting and exploitative usage of humans. It became embanked, diverted for irrigation and its floodplain was drained and substantially dried out. Papyrus vanished from much of its former range and many of the examples which can be seen in Egypt now are derived from reintroduced stock.

In another thread through history, the papyrus sedge has been moved around the world as an exotic ornamental plant, escaping into the wild in Hawai'i, California, Louisiana and Florida, where it has become an invasive alien, dominating many native species.

Around 2,000 years ago, papyrus began to be superseded by parchment, a more robust form of writing substrate made from prepared animal skins; these were able to be bound into forms recognisable as books, aiding their

The falcon, seen here on a papyrus from *Ramose's Book of the Dead*, represents the god Sokar, symbolic of royal rebirth and confirmation of regal power. The head pattern suggests that this is Barbary Falcon, a close relative of Peregrine.

repeated use and storage. Few papyri or the scrolls into which they were compiled survive in legible form today, as they were easily compromised by both humidity and dryness, as well as being rough to write and draw on, limiting their use.

Papyrus has a basal role in the history of ornithological publishing, being the original source of printed and written media as we know them. The actual reproduction of writing in the form of printing would have to wait for another 1,400 years, however.

4 : Lysippe's bust
of Aristotle

c. 330 BC

Birds must have always had an important role in human affairs, not least in the uses of their meat and eggs for food, their depredations on crops and livestock, their feathers for clothing and decoration, and their migration and dispersal as an indication of changing seasons and weather.

This last point in particular may well have inspired those of a philosophical bent, and it is in what remains of the work of one of the greatest ancient Greek writers and teachers, mostly preserved as medieval manuscripts, that we find the first written descriptions and musings upon natural history and the subject's most notable signifiers – birds.

Aristotle lived from 384 to 322 BC, and was the first known writer to undertake what we would recognise as a systematic study of birds, though his legacy also includes a truly polymathic range of subjects from geology to poetry, physics to logic, and theatre to pioneering work in zoology. From the point of view of the modern birder, it is notable that much of his research was original and took place in the Aegan on or around the migration hot-spot island of Lesvos, producing enduring compilations of observation, empiricism and myth entitled *Inquiries on Animals, On the Generation of Animals* and *On the Parts of Animals*.

Though they were informed as much by hearsay as study, Aristotle took great heed of the field experience of farmers, fishermen and hunters, and their insight into the songs, food, distribution and seasonality of birds. He also classified the known species according to the form of their feet (an ecologically logical start point) and the nature of their food, dividing them into seed-eaters, insect-eaters and meat-eaters. He was astute enough to realise that the physiology and anatomy of birds are informed by their environment, noting that size was influenced by climate and that some birds were altitudinal migrants, that different plumages existed at different times of the year, and even the parallels between reptile scales and feathers.

However, he also wrote that swallows, storks, woodpigeons and starlings hibernated after shedding their feathers, and that the Black Redstart moulted its plumage to become Robins. Swallows were also believed to be able to heal punctured eyeballs and nightjars to suck blood and goats' milk. Aristotle was, though, able to refute some of the myths of the day, such as the belief that vultures hatched out of the ground.

The original bronze bust of Aristotle by Lysippe has been lost,
and, like most of what we know about the master philosopher,
has been passed down as an Imperial Roman copy.

Aristotle was a giant of his time, but many other works of natural history were written in ancient times, and are mostly now lost. However, the knowledge contained in more than 2,000 of these was compiled by the Roman historian, Pliny the Elder (Gaius Plinius Secundus, 23 to 79 AD), whose *Natural History* contains much early ornithology, particularly in its 10th volume. His classification begins with Ostrich, which he believed to be closely related to ungulate mammals, and Common Crane. The mythical Phoenix was included, Pliny raising doubts about its existence, though he still maintained that some migratory birds hibernated (a belief that persisted well into the 19th century in western Europe).

Pliny's encyclopaedia, along with the anonymous Second Century text *Physiologus*, shows that empirical science was gradually developing almost universally in the great ancient civilisations. However, the rise to power of dogmatic religious authority would virtually scupper this until the 15th century, when the ancient texts would be rediscovered and help fuel more radical and widespread scientific enquiry, and with it revolutions in zoology and the origin of ornithology as we know it today.

5 : Gutenberg printing press

1440

After little advancement of science during medieval times, scholars had some catching up to do. The first to seriously assimilate the findings of Aristotle and Pliny from the remaining translations of Arab, Greek and Roman precursors was William Turner.

A doctor and Northumberland native, Turner published the first printed book solely devoted to birds in 1544, with the unwieldy full title of *Avium praecipuarum, quarum apud Plinium et Aristotelem mentio est, brevis et succincta historia* — a short and succinct history of birds, most of which are mentioned in Pliny and Aristotle (see pages 18-19). Even as early as 1538, he had published his attempt at a full list of English flora and fauna, and such personal and public inventories are in some ways still widespread in modern birding.

A few other authors had briefly summarised ornithological knowledge beforehand within broader works, but *Avium praecipuarum* (written in exile, as Turner was a religious non-conformist) was a unique summary of ornithological knowledge at the time. This turning point in bird studies would not have been possible without a whole concatenation of previous communication innovations.

Mass-produced paper replaced parchment when water-powered paper mills were introduced around 1282, though paper had been manufactured in some form since the second century AD, initially in China. Bound books had evolved from Greek codices, and were commonplace in monasteries in the first few centuries of the Christian era in the West, and even some secular works were included in the libraries that began to be assembled during the sixth century.

The real revelation for written communication came with Johannes Gutenburg's invention of the printing press around 1440 — for the first time it was possible to produce more than one copy of a work at the same time. This innovation was swiftly followed by a publishing industry which provided investment of capital and sales to a market of consumers, albeit only the few who had the money and education to be able to read. A variety of coloured inks enabled books to be profusely illustrated from the start.

Although he confused Bittern with White Pelican, it was also the inclusion of many of Turner's own observations that made *Avium praecipuarum* a great leap forward, and the 16th century began to provide learned tomes for and by natural historians from then onwards, with works by Pierre Belon (France, 1555), Conrad

Printing presses, like this one shown in an old woodcut, are still
used in a similar form by limited edition and art publishers today,
emphasising their revolutionary capacity when first invented.

Gessner (Germany, 1555), Volcher Coiter (Holland, 1575) and Ulisse Aldrovandi (Italy, 1603) in quick succession.

While much of the content of these first published works was apocryphal or folkloric, more was derived from field observations of European birds, and also from the first global forays of the Age of Exploration in Elizabethan times. With information and objects from the wider world pouring into Europe, the religious stranglehold over science and philosophy loosened and gradually allowed the first strained breaths of reason to be expelled through its fractured filter.

It is with the publication of Turner's avian magnum opus, the first true bird book, that Britain can perhaps lay claim to being the birthplace of birding.

6 : Raphael's Madonna of the Goldfinch

1505

Little actual ornithology, at least as we would recognise it, occurred during the Middle Ages, though falconry texts occasionally went into detail about the behaviour of birds of prey, and recognised that many raptors migrated rather than hibernated, as was thought by Aristotle.

Though birds were widely represented in Byzantine and Gothic art, it was in the Renaissance eras — with pioneering science, exploration and the dissemination of the printed word — that artistic skill and accuracy of observation combined to produce many artefacts of bird species rendered in detail, and imbued with symbolic religious, folkloric and sometimes even biological meaning.

Common in European renaissance art is the Goldfinch, usually held in the hands of the infant Christ to imply the fragility of the soul or the resurrection and sacrifice, and present in at least 486 devotional paintings by more than 250 artists. Europe was constantly under the threat of plague between the 14th and 17th centuries, and this had the effect of imbuing the Goldfinch with a more portentous role: that of healer or redeemer.

Many other accurate renditions of bird species are present in the flowering of Christian art, including the Peacock (more accurately called Indian Peafowl) to variously represent pride or the all-watching eyes of the Church (due to the eye-like patterns on its elongated tail-coverts); White Stork representing spring, piety or chastity; eagles symbolising Jesus himself; and most obviously, doves representing peace and chastity.

Hand-in-hand with Renaissance art, though usually accompanied by less accurately illustrated birds, were the first bird books (see pages 28-29). Among these early publications was the first avian anatomical work, *Zootomia Democritaea* (1645) by Marco Aurelio Severino, which compared the anatomy of birds to demonstrate the variety of Creation.

This, and other published advances in embryology and physiology, would have a profound effect on the classification of birds, as would parallel refinements in the taxidermy of bird specimens. However, early explorers were able to bring back the skins of numerous exotic creatures, as well as the occasional live specimen, for public display. This almost certainly explains the zoogeographical hodge-podge of artists like Roelant Savery, with his Ostrich from Africa and his Scarlet Macaws from South America in *Vögel in einer Landschaft* (1622), or the incongruous meeting of Purple

The Goldfinch in Raphael's masterwork symbolises the crucifixion of Christ, by virtue of the bird's red head markings. Legend says that the bird was splashed by blood as it removed a thorn from the Messiah's crown.

Swamphen and Surf Scoter (from the freshwater marshes of North Africa and the inshore seas of Atlantic North America, respectively) in Peter Paul Rubens and Jan Breughel's *The Garden of Eden* (c.1617).

Renaissance art was a direct influence on the more literal and figurative artists that followed, many of whom began to paint and draw beautifully detailed and scientifically accurate avian portraits. These were often intended to act as visual appendices to zoological descriptions or museum catalogues, or frequently to be sold to collectors and wealthy aficionados.

7 : Bird-nesting pot

c.1600-1699

Humans have always enjoyed a commensal relationship with certain species that are able to exploit man-made structures or waste products for nest sites or food.

In Britain, a suburban house in recent times will probably have played host to some or all of House Martin, Common Swift, Jackdaw, Starling and House Sparrow, while the back garden would add anything between 10 and 20 more breeding and feeding species to this list.

Whether through sentiment or the need for dietary supplement, people have historically encouraged birds to nest on or near their abodes by providing artificial nest sites. Such objects have been recorded at least since Roman times.

The medieval period saw clay pots for House Sparrows and Starlings being erected in Holland, principally as their chicks were considered delicacies. The late 17th century bird pot illustrated here was dug up at Rectory Grove in Clapham, London, in 1980, and would originally have been hung on the outside of a building to encourage House Sparrows.

Only 50 to 60 such pots are known to archaeologists, and they date from anywhere around 1500 to 1850. In Britain, they have only been unearthed in London and may have spread from the continent via trade across the English Channel and North Sea. A typical artificial nest has a 'robbery hole' at its back, enabling the householder to take eggs or nestlings for the working class cooking pot, but several have also been excavated at wealthier houses, and it is speculated that live adult sparrows may also have been captured through the robbery holes, and used in falconry.

Nestboxes put up merely for the pleasure of encouraging local birds or seeing them raise their young are not recorded until the 19th century, when the first known wooden boxes, recognisable to the modern eye and designed for Tawny Owl, Sand Martin, Jackdaw and Starling, were put up by the English naturalist Charles Waterton in Yorkshire.

The first use of nestboxes for scientific research was in the early 20th century, when they were used in America for ornithological studies of the House Wren.

The widespread deforestation of most western countries – and further afield in modern times – and the management of remaining woodlands (which often involves removing old or rotten timber) has depleted rural areas of many natural nest sites. Nestboxes now have an essential purpose as places where declining species can rebuild

This 17th century pot was excavated in
Clapham, London, and would likely have
been used to provide a home for House
Sparrows destined for the cooking pot.

their numbers; groups of boxes for sparrows,
or even whole artificial colonies for communal
species like Sand Martin, are now constructed.

Modern nestboxes come in numerous shapes
and sizes, and are manufactured from many
different materials, including wood, cement,
hardboard, plastic, metal and even a German-
invented combination of sawdust, clay and
concrete patented as 'woodcrete'. Their form
has been adapted for birds as small as Blue Tits
and as large as Great Grey Owls, while they
also provide roosting sites not only for
wintering birds like Wren and Treecreeper, but
also mammals like bats, dormice and Harvest
Mice, and insects such as bumblebees.

In Britain, the types in most common use
are small, sealed oblong boxes with either a
round hole for an entrance – suitable for tits,
sparrows, Pied Flycatchers and Starlings – or a
rectangular open front for species like Robin
or Spotted Flycatcher. Large oblong boxes with
wide openings are used by Common Kestrel or
Stock Dove, while some species of owls prefer
tubular affairs. Shallow clay cups or trays
attract Swallows or encourage House Martins
when placed under rafters and eaves.

8 : First scientific paper

1665

Before experimental results become accepted, or before a species is defined as a discrete entity by the scientific community (and consequently birders), conclusions are published formally as a paper in a scientific journal.

Until the 17th century, however, the results of scientific endeavours were often kept private, written in Latin or code, announced in the form of anagrams, or compiled into a magnum opus. The almost simultaneous publication of the first issues of the *Journal des Scavans* in France and the British *Philosophical Transactions of the Royal Society* in January and March 1665 changed this; both are still going strong. They rapidly established strict writing and data presentation protocols that still apply today and, though this can make for a dry read, the interchangeable style enables scientists to replicate, compare and evaluate results internationally and through time.

As truly disciplined academic inquiry was itself only just emerging during the 17th century, the advent of formal scientific publishing helped shape its development. Research had to conform to the formulation of a hypothesis, the laying out of a repeatable method to test that hypothesis, a concise summary and interpretation of the results, and a conclusion. The contents of papers have varied little since, and nor has the formality of having the contents reviewed by anonymous expert peers before publication.

The naming of a species has its own precise protocol within the journal system, a process referred to as 'alpha taxonomy', which involves publishing a detailed diagnostic description in a scientific journal, as well as depositing type specimens within a museum or collection.

Formally, an ornithologist (or, indeed, other biologist) naming a new species is called an author and is expected to be familiar with the majority of the published literature and extant forms and their accepted classification. In the case of a bird new to science, the paper in which the description of the type specimen is published should also contain a physical run-down of the main features of male, female and immature plumages, as well as vocalisations if possible and relevant, and also the circumstances under which the bird was 'collected' and any field observations that were made.

Most species are visually separable from each other, but as many a modern birder will realise, just because a form is identifiable in the field doesn't make it a species, and

PHILOSOPHICAL
TRANSACTIONS:
GIVING SOME
ACCOMPT
OF THE PRESENT
Undertakings, Studies, and Labours
OF THE
INGENIOUS
IN MANY
CONSIDERABLE PARTS
OF THE
WORLD.

Vol I.
For Anno 1665, and 1666.

In the SAVOY,
Printed by T. N. for John Martyn at the Bell, a little with-
out Temple-Bar, and James Alleftry in Duck-Lane,
Printers to the Royal Society.

In 1665, the Royal Society of London for Improving Natural Knowledge published the first issue of its journal, having been granted permission by Charles II, and has broken the news of many of the latest scientific discoveries consistently ever since.

conversely some species are not easily separable from their near relations by physical appearance. The definition of the term 'species' itself is constantly debated, with no conception of the term applying in all circumstances.

It may all seem a little confusing, as well as dusty and unexciting, to the field birder, but without the methods and protocols first established almost 250 years ago, tricky birds would be even harder to put a name to in the field. The struggle to figure out what exactly we are looking at continues …

9 : *Ornithologiae Libri Tres* by John Ray and Francis Willughby

1676

In 1676, the naturalist John Ray published a book he had co-written under the sole name of Francis Willughby, in tribute to his dead friend, though it is of little doubt now that Ray was also a major author. Its 441 pages in three volumes contained the first systematic attempt to comprehensively itemise the British avifauna. It encompassed about 230 species, though some foreign forms were mentioned and several names were sometimes used for single species. However, it had an unprecedented scientific rigour for its time and classified birds according to their detailed physical characteristics, including plumage. A few other lists had been attempted in the two previous centuries, including a fairly full but somewhat folkloric British list compiled by Christopher Merrett just 10 years earlier, suspected to have inspired Ray and Willughby to improve upon it.

The two ornithologists could hardly have come from more disparate backgrounds, with Ray the son of an Essex blacksmith whose Cambridge education was paid for by a philanthropic clergyman, while Willughby came from land-owning aristocratic stock.

Despite Ray's social 'inferiority', it was Willughby who came under the influence of Ray's charisma and mental discipline as they began working together after meeting at Trinity College. Ray, though ordained, was a religious non-conformist and resigned his clerical status to travel Europe with his new-found companion, and during their travels they collected specimens and dissected them on the road. They kept detailed notes of their examinations of species like Great Bustard and Black Stork, observing such features as feathering, musculature and parasites.

Ray was not financially secure and had to work as a private tutor (sometimes for Willughby's children) to raise funds for his travels and studies. The somewhat frail Willughby died at the young age of 37, leaving Ray a then-significant annuity of £60. The early death spurred Ray into writing up their notes as *Ornithologiae Libri Tres* — literally three books of ornithology — published in Latin and containing a surprising quantity of knowledge. They used a binary classification, dividing their subjects into landbirds and waterbirds, and using their observed physical characteristics to further subdivide into classes.

Landbirds included crooked-beaked diurnal birds of prey (including shrikes and birds-of-

TAB XII

Lanius sive Monedula
The Jack daw

Coracias Aldrov
The Cornish Chough

Pica varia seu caudata
The Magpie or Piannet

Pica glandaria
The Jay

The corvid plate from *Ornithologiae Libri Tres*; Willughby
died of pleurisy as the work was in progress, but Ray was
able to see it through to publication and success.

paradise), nocturnal birds of prey and parrots, and straight-beaked ratites. Waterbirds were divided into marshland species with dagger-like bills, crooked- or straight-billed waders, those waders with medium-sized bills, and plovers (with short bills). A further waterbird division was that of open water species, including groups for Eurasian Coot and Moorhen, flamingo and Avocet, auks, cormorants and Gannet, and more. It wasn't a bad start, though some names are confusing in a modern context, and others, like 'arsfoot' for grebes and divers, amusingly prosaic.

It seems likely, on Ray's own admission, that Willughby was the more meticulous observer; Ray entered his detailed plumage notes into the book almost untouched. Both can be looked on as the fathers of modern bird studies and observation, and they made many important advances.

However, the first truly logically systematic list of bird would be established by a Swedish botanist in the following century (see pages 32-33).

10 : Stuffed Dodo at the Horniman Museum, London

c. 1700

Stuffed birds — and a stuffed Dodo in particular — are signifiers of many aspects of the human treatment and discovery of the world of birds. The craft of taxidermy underwent an explosion from the 16th century until the early 20th century, though methods of animal skin preservation such as mummification go back at least a few thousand years.

Specimens were, and remain, of paramount importance for anatomical and taxonomic studies, while stuffed animals and trophies were also of great commercial value for most of the last 500 years or so. The skins of extinct birds are among the most valuable financially and taxonomically, and the causes and outcomes of the extinction of a species are the subject of thousands of scientific papers and much debate. Even the very finality of the extirpation of a unique life form has only been widely understood and appreciated for 150 years or so.

The start of the modern cycle of extinction is often dated to 1600, and it is the 17th century which saw the discovery and demise of that most charismatic of columbiforms, the Dodo. The large, grey-brown, flightless, ground-nesting island endemic weighed about 20kg and lived mainly on a diet of fruit. It was part of a speciose and bizarre Mascarene island fauna, much of which we are only discovering now, and most of which has been destroyed completely or only survives in highly threatened remnant or human-dependent populations.

Though discovered by Dutch sailors in 1598 on the Indian Ocean island of Mauritius, the Dodo wasn't described until 1606 and had diverged so much from its pigeon ancestors (DNA analysis has shown the closest is likely to have been Nicobar Pigeon from the East Indian islands) that it was given its own family, Raphidae, along with the solitaires of neighbouring islands, and was initially believed to have affinities to the ratites, swans or vultures.

By 1700 at the latest, it was extinct, killed off for food (though reputedly it was only barely palatable) and by the depredations of dogs, pigs and other alien mammals; for the first time in its evolutionary history, the Dodo had had enemies. The species' passing was largely unsung until the late 19th century, despite its remarkable size and appearance, and unique ecological role on the island. Its behaviour, habits and even its true appearance

While the Dodo 'specimen' at the Horniman Museum – and in several other museums – is the epitome of how people imagine the species, it is in fact both fake and conjectural.

have had to be pieced together from contemporary explorers' accounts and drawings, which contain all the inaccuracies of the time liberally mixed up with accurate observations, along with a few partial dessicated specimens from the time and recently excavated bones from caves and bogs on Mauritius, including a whole skeleton in 2007.

The bird itself was frequently depicted as ungainly, somewhat like an obese chicken, but it seems likely that this impression was gained from poorly executed drawings and badly stuffed specimens. Research has shown that it is likely to have been much slimmer than is traditionally thought, and was a quite active running species.

This particular 'specimen' from London's Horniman Museum underlines the bird's ignominious demise, as no genuine stuffed Dodo exists anywhere – this model is formed from plaster casts of a genuine preserved head and feet, and a manufactured body covered with swan and goose feathers. Even more pathetically, real feathered chicken wings have been attached and the tail has been formed out of Ostrich feathers. It was made by the taxidermist Rowland Ward's company in 1938.

The Dodo must surely stand as both a monument to the uniqueness of island evolution, and an icon of remembrance as to what can happen to the dozens of isolated evolutionary hot-spots around the globe should we falter in our attempts to preserve them.

11 : *Systema Naturae* (10th edition) by Carolus Linnaeus

1758

Whether you're a birder or an ornithologist, it's always useful to know where a species perches on the tree of life. We need a rational and logical classification system in which to do this, and since we now know that all bird species have evolved from a series of common ancestors, it would be logical for that classification to follow evolutionary history as closely as possible, but also for it to be 'linear' to be comprehensible.

But linearity and historical reality are contradictory in evolutionary terms. We know that the story of evolution is continuously branching; some sort of sense can be introduced by trying to put the order of the branching of the major groups – justified orders and families – in a roughly chronological sequence.

After Ray and Willughby's valiant attempts to classify birds into physical types and major habitats, the problem remained that the manner in which species originated was still unknown. However, the way plants and animals were ordered was about to be revolutionised by an ingenious expedient: they would be given names that described an organism's place and relationships in a hierarchy in simple terms. This would involve a two-part scientific name to indicate to scientists and the science-literate

laity exactly where it was thought an organism lay in the grand biological scheme.

Scientific names as we know them today – the binomial of a genus and a species qualifier – were first established in a consistent way by Swedish botanist Carolus Linnaeus (born Carl von Linné) in the 10th edition of his *Systema Naturae* way back in 1758. Previously, organisms had been identified by unwieldy and lengthy descriptive Latin phrases. The Linnaean hierarchy and genus-species system has been retained ever since, with the addition of a sometimes still controversial trinomial for subspecies.

Dissatisfied with the then current mode of classifying living organisms, Linnaeus gradually developed his more intuitive system based on morphological similarity, beginning with the stamens and pistils of flowering plants in what was termed his sexual system. Written during a three-year stay in The Netherlands from 1735 to 1739, the *Systema* was under constant revision, and the 10th edition also featured prescient innovations such as the placement of whales in the class Mammalia, and the classification of humans with monkeys.

Linnaeus – no slouch at self-promotion – was reputed to have said more than once that

The 10th edition of *Systema Naturae* listed 564 species of bird – including many then recently discovered tropical forms – classified according to the general characters of their beaks and feet.

'God created, Linnaeus organised', and his hierarchy of kingdoms, classes, orders, genera, species and 'varieties' has passed down the years relatively intact. It remains both easy to understand and the standard method of classifying plants and animals to demonstrate their relationships to one another, despite the development of the theory of evolution and our detailed and growing knowledge of the genome.

12 : Gilbert White's *The Natural History and Antiquities of Selborne*

1789

A batch of letters written by a country clergyman to noted zoologists Thomas Pennant and Daines Barrington has remained a classic nature book since it was first published in 1789. An outstanding amateur ornithologist, the author, Gilbert White, can also be seen as the first 'patch birder', observing the changes and details of his parish and making many discoveries along the way.

After a 12-year clerical career in southern England and The Midlands, White inherited his father's house in Selborne, Hampshire, where he took charge of the parish as curate. A keen gardener, his meticulous and methodical record-keeping of the annual weather, temperature and crops he planted soon spread into a general but deep curiosity about the natural world in his local area.

He began a correspondence with two other learned gentlemen, Pennant (an eminent zoologist) and Barrington (barrister and Fellow of the Royal Society), exchanging opinions about the plants and animals around them, drawn — unusually for the time — from observations in life rather than impressions gleaned from specimens, as biologists were then generally wont to do.

These letters — erudite, insightful and well-written — were published in book form in 1789 as *The Natural History and Antiquities of Selborne*, and underline White's appreciation of the inter-connectedness of all living things, as well as his sharp eye as a field observer. He is often mentioned as the first ecologist, and with the archive of his continuous empirical data as well as his philosophical and observational musings, this opinion is hard to refute.

Of the plentiful information published in the book, perhaps the most appreciated by birders was his field separation — without optical aids — of Chiffchaff, Willow Warbler and Wood Warbler by call, song and appearance, avoiding the contemporary vogue for specimen collection. Even today, the first two species still cause frequent identification problems. With this profound distinguishing of three then-common small birds, White set out exactly the kind of observations that would attract many people to the hobby of birding, and also recruit others into academic ornithology and the natural sciences.

White was also among the first to speculate that Swallows migrated, despite the traditional but unfounded belief that they hibernated, noting in a letter to Barrington in June 1769 that "Most soft-billed birds live on insects, and

This detail from a 1920 stained glass window in Selbourne
church, created and installed by G. Gascoigne and Son,
shows a few of the 82 species mentioned in White's letters,
all of which are incorporated into the design.

not on grain and seed; and therefore at the end of summer they retire", after noting all the local summer visitors' arrival and departure dates. He also thought about why the numbers of his local Common Swifts remained static every year, despite their breeding success, raising the questions of their destination every autumn, their survival potential and the availability of nest sites. His reputation, even in his own lifetime, led to biologist John Latham naming White's Thrush in his honour.

The accuracy of the information contained in *Selborne* and White's diaries and notebooks remains useful today, as these, along with the diaries of William Markwick in Battle, Sussex, have provided unique historical comparative data on the phenology – that is, the study of the effect of climate on the seasonal cycles of animals and plants – of more than 440 species over the 25-year period between 1768 and 1793. Such data are essential in judging the reality and effects of climate change, perhaps humanity's most pressing global issue.

Selborne was probably the first of an eventual myriad of natural history and birding memoirs, and certainly one of the most lyrical, accurate and detailed. The book has never been out of print and remains an object lesson in meticulous systematic note-taking and record-keeping.

13 : 18th-century wood carving knife

1797

An important and aesthetically interesting side road in the history of illustration was the use of woodcuts, and later linocuts, to produce multiple printed renditions of birds. Central to that medium was the carvers' knife, ingeniously used to fashion a relief design in wood, onto which ink was applied to create a 'raised' illustration which was the mirror-image of the resulting printed piece.

Perhaps the most important woodcut artist was also an ornithologist. Thomas Bewick (1753-1828) was a trained engraver from Northumberland, and his brilliance as a woodcarver led to the self-publication of the *History of British Birds*, one of the early great works on Britain's avifauna. This two-volume work, divided into landbirds and waterbirds and partly following Ray and Willughby's classification (see pages 28-29), was created and published between 1797 and 1804. It contained information partly derived from Bewick's own observations on rural excursions, as well as the writings of naturalists of the day such as Gilbert White (see pages 34-35).

Bewick's methods were innovatory, using hardwoods like box instead of the then traditional softwoods like pine, and carving against the grain with metal engravers' more fine-gauged tools like the burin, a needle-shaped tool with a V-shaped cutting end. Despite the stylised appearance of the resulting black-and-white ink prints, there is much ornithological accuracy in his work. Though not discovered by the artist, Bewick's Swan was named in his honour.

The techniques are kept alive today in their original form, and by carvers using matrices like PVC or resin, or, in the case of the most famous modern practitioner, Robert Gillmor, as linocuts. In this technique, first developed in 1905, a sheet of linoleum – generally manufactured from solidified pine resin (aka rosin) or linseed oil – is mounted on a wooden block, essentially as a substitute for wood.

Artists as respected and varied as Escher, Matisse and Picasso used the technique, but in the natural world it is best known in Gillmor's deceptively primitive primary-coloured illustrations for the jackets of the Collins New Naturalist series. A distinguished birder and artist who co-founded the Society of Wildlife Artists in 1964, Gillmor produces illustrations to this day and in 2012 he was commissioned to produce a set of stamps for the Royal Mail.

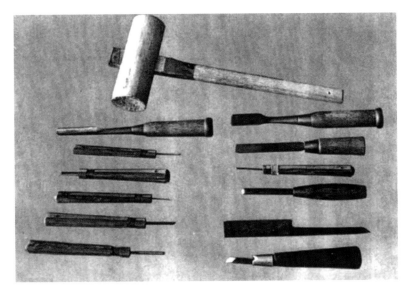

This selection of wood carving tools (above) is similar to those that would have
been used by Bewick to create his master engraving of the Barn Owl (top),
included in his *History of British Birds* (1797–1804).

14 : Hummingbird cabinet of curiosities, Natural History Museum, London

19th century

Collections of natural history specimens were not always the preserve of museums, and much of the credit for the discovery and spread of knowledge of biodiversity belongs initially with private collectors, as the great age of exploration flowered hand-in-hand with exploitative colonialism.

The first 'cabinets of curiosity' were created in the 16th century all over imperial Europe, and were collections of interesting and worldly objects, both natural and man-made, intended to inspire thought and discussion, as well as to display the owner's power, knowledge and reach. Usually display cabinets, they were also sometimes entire rooms with then uncategorised natural objects, ranging from fossils, ancient statues, unusual tools and musical instruments to skulls, horns, pressed flowers, seashells and, of course, stuffed birds, all arranged according to the aesthetics of their owner.

As the world became more penetrated by western discovery, natural history specimens were a great source of the intrigue and interest of such cabinets. The first known illustrated collection dedicated to this subject was a 1599 engraving in *Dell'Historia Naturale* by Ferranto Imperato of Naples, which shows audacious use of every surface of the room to display artefacts, including the ceiling, which holds an alligator among many suspended trophies.

Other earlier collections were described in the literature and also served as repositories for scientific description and endeavour. Such a cabinet was that of Ole Worm of Aarhus, Denmark, who – despite several dubious specimens of mythological creatures – was able to correctly assign a long spiral tusk to Narwhal, rather than fancifully to a Unicorn, as most people thought. Worm's catalogue served as a scientific resource, too, and showed that birds-of-paradise possessed feet, a fact hitherto unknown until his writings in the 17th century, as specimens were usually prepared *in situ* without feet.

Worm was contemporary with Sir Hans Sloane, a London doctor who had catalogues and collections which included many bird specimens, and these formed the central collection of the British Museum upon his death. Other labelled, sourced and annotated private accumulations founded collections at the Ashmolean Museum, Oxford, and others across Europe, creating a foundation for taxonomic studies that continue to the present day.

Hummingbirds, like the many specimens in this impressive display at the
Natural History Museum, were – along with parrots and birds-of-paradise
– highly prized by collectors and owners of cabinets of curiosity.

As such collections held materials that were more correctly identified, their owners specialised and many 19th-century cabinets became solely dedicated to certain groups, such as coral, or invertebrate fossils, or (as in the photograph above), hummingbirds. These New World nectar specialists were ideal for the moneyed collector, being beautiful, manageable in size, and speciose, and became highly popular among the ranks of collectors. Notable for the number and variety of specimens, this particular hummingbird collection is believed to have belonged to William Bullock, one of the first curators of the museum, who was almost obsessed with the family.

15 : Montagu's *Ornithological Dictionary*

1802

As ornithological studies became more frequent among scientists and gentlemen, much knowledge began to accumulate in scientific papers, nature books and memoirs. The way was open for someone adept in these matters to compile and summarise what was known, as the 19th century got into its stride and publications of quality began to become the standard.

The first summary of ornithological knowledge about behaviour, anatomy, plumage and distribution was published by George Montagu, a legendarily meticulous aristocrat and a pedant whose work thus became somewhat more reliable than the more imaginative scholars of his day. This attention to detail enabled him, like Gilbert White just before him, to add new species to the British list. These of course included the eponymous harrier, more common in the 19th century than it is now, but also he was astute enough to recognise Roseate Tern and Cirl Bunting by their variably subtle respective differences from Common and Arctic Terns and Yellowhammer.

Montagu amassed information about birds by personal observation and, again like White, by correspondence with fellow specimen collectors; he could be viewed as one of the first listers, being very keen to obtain stuffed individuals of every possible British species.

His *Ornithological Dictionary* (1802) was published in two parts, often the case where books were funded by well-heeled subscribers, but he also added a supplement in 1813. Species were listed in alphabetical order, questions of identification were specifically addressed, and Montagu was able to point out that some birds considered different species were in fact mere alternative plumages of the same bird. For the first time the characters that placed birds in a single genus were itemised, and the dictionary was very much an erudite precursor to the works of later authors like Yarrell, Witherby and numerous other ornithologists, right up to Cramp and Perrins' multi-volume *The Handbook of the Birds of Europe, North Africa and the Middle East* (1977-94), still the regional standard in its recently discontinued DVD-ROM form known as *BWPi* (2006).

market, in 1812-13, said to have been taken in a decoy near Malden, Essex. It is a native of Eastern Siberia. Its call is a sort of clucking.*

BIRD.—"The external parts of a bird which require to be noticed and distinguished by the naturalist, are the head, neck, body, wings, tail, and legs; which parts again are subdivided more or less minutely, according to the taste of various writers on the subject. I think it will be useful to younger naturalists to give an outline engraving to assist them in naming these several parts."

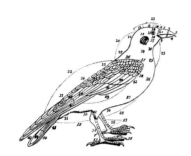

1. MAXILLA SUPERIOR, the upper mandible of the bill.
2. MAXILLA INFERIOR, the lower mandible of the bill.
3. CULMEN, the ridge of the bill.
4. GONYS, the angle or point of the under mandible.
5. DERTRUM, the hook of the bill.
6. NARES, the nostrils.
7. MESORHINIUM, the upper ridge of the bill.
8. LORUM, the bone, a naked space at the base of the bill.
9. MENTUM, the chin.
10. FRONS, the forehead.

11. VERTEX, the crown of the head.
12. SINCIPUT, the hinder part of the head.
13. CAPISTRUM, the face.
14. SUPERCILIUM, the eye-brow.
15. REGIO OPHTHALMICA, the region of the eye.
16. TEMPORA, the temples.
17. GENA, the cheek.
18. REGIO PAROTICA, the parts about the ear.
19. COLLUM, the neck.
20. CERVIX, the hinder part of the neck.
21. NUCHA, the nape of the neck.
22. AUCHENIUM, the under nape of the neck.

D 2

Kestrel.

KAE.—A name for the Jackdaw.
KAMTSCHATKA TERN.—A name for the Black Tern.
KATABELLA.—A name for the Hen Harrier.
KATE.—A name for the Hawfinch.
KATOGLE.—A name for the Eagle Owl.
KENTISH PLOVER.—A variety of the Ring Plover.
KESTREL (*Falco tinnunculus*, LINNÆUS.)
*Falco Tinnunculus, *Lath.* Ind. Orn. 1. p. 41. t. 98.—*Gmel.* Syst. 1. p. 278. 16 *Raii,* Syn. pl. 16. 16.—*Will.* p. 50. t. 5.—*Meyer,* Tasschenb. 1. p. 62.—Falco Tinnunculus alaudarius, *Gmel.* Syst. p. 279.—Accipiter alaudarius, *Briss.* 1. p. 379. 22.—La Cresserelle, *Buff.* Ois. 1. p. 379.—*Ib.* pl. Enl. 401. old male, and 471. the young of the year.—Faucon Cresserelle, *Temm.* Man. d'Orn. 1. p. 29. Turm-falke, *Bechst.* Taschenb. Deut. 1. p. 37.—Kestrel, Stannel, or Windho-ver, *Will.* (Angl.) p. 84. t. 5.—Kestrel, Br. Zool. 1. No. 60.—*Ib.* fol. p. 68. t. A.—Arct. Zool. 2. p. 226. N.—*Lath.* Syn. 1. p. 94. 79.—*Ib.* Supp. 2. p. 25.—*Lewin's* Br. Birds, 1. t. 19. Mand. F.—*Mont.* Orn. Dict.—*Walc.* Syn. 1. t. 19. *Pult.* Cat. Dorset, p. 3.—Lew's Faun. Orcad. p. 37.—*Don.* Br. Birds, 3. t. 51.—*Shaw's* Zool. 7. p. 179.—*Haye's* Br. Birds, t. 4.—*Bewick's* Br. Birds, 1. p. 38. & 40. Mand. F.—*Flem.* Br. Anim. p. 50.—*Selby,* pl. 17. & 17*. p. 43.

Provincial.—Kastril, Stonegall, Creshawk.*

The male of this species of falcon weighs about seven ounces; length thirteen inches. Bill lead-colour; cere yellow; irides dusky and large. The crown of the head is of a fine cinereous grey; throat whitish;

T 2

Despite being scientifically described by Linnaeus in 1758, it was Montagu who discovered his eponymous harrier species (above) breeding in Britain, resulting in its English name. His innovative dictionary included standard nomenclature for avian anatomy (top) and an alphabetical list of known species (above right).

16 : *Observations on the Brumal Retreat of the Swallow* by Thomas Forster

1808

After a birder has begun to identify birds in the field, and has accumulated often several field guides, the next step in many cases is to investigate a single group of birds, particularly hard-to-identify species. Traditionally this will involve a hefty cash investment in an ornithological monograph, an often doorstep-sized study of a single group or species in which the detailed labours of many observers and scientists over many years are combined to give as comprehensive a survey of current knowledge as possible.

The classic monographs for birders are those published by Collins in the robust and expansive New Naturalist series and also the highly collectible T & A D Poyser tomes, but new additions are constantly being released by other publishers too. This is a not a modern phenomenon, however – the history of recognisable bird monographs goes back to the 19th century, the first arguably being *Observations on the Brumal Retreat of the Swallow* by Thomas Forster (1808). This was a small volume in which the author presented evidence that Swallows migrated rather than hibernated in the mud at the bottom of lakes, including observations made by seafarers off the coast of Senegal who had seen the species there in

October. He also itemised the known species of swallow, erroneously including Common Swift among them.

The great bird artists of the 19th century also published serious, copiously and beautifully illustrated monographs on popular bird groups, and sales of these expensive and limited edition tomes helped counter the costs of scientific illustration and documentation of some of that era's expeditions of discovery. Gould is covered on pages 54–55, but special mention must go to Edward Lear's *Illustrations of the Family of Psittacidae* (1832) which featured 42 exquisitely and painstakingly accurate illustraions of parrots from private collections and zoos, a critical success but financial failure.

The accumulation of observations of behaviour, physiology and evolution of different bird groups during the late 19th century and throughout the 20th century, combined with the growing popularity of birdwatching, meant that the market was ripe for thorough summaries of information about favoured bird groups, and publishers began to publish many single-species guides after the Second World War.

Since then, extensive and comprehensive family and order guides have become popular,

OBSERVATIONS

ON THE

BRVMAL RETREAT

OF THE

SWALLOW.

TO WHICH IS ANNEXED

A COPIOVS INDEX

TO MANY PASSAGES RELATING TO THIS BIRD,

IN THE WORKS OF ANCIENT AND MODERN AUTHORS.

BY

THOMAS FORSTER, F. L. S.

AUTHOR OF

"RESEARCHES ABOUT ATMOSPHERIC PHAENOMENA"—

"DIOSEMEA OF ARATUS,"—etc.

FOURTH EDITION, CORRECTED AND ENLARGED.

[This Edition is not published separately.]

1814.

'Brumal' means relating to the winter, and it was Forster who established
that Swallows migrated to Africa, partly from making a chronology of
the dates of accounts of the species from travellers.

while taking advantage of photographic skills to supplement painted plates and field observations has allowed the plumage variations of each species in a family guide to be copiously illustrated in the early 21st century. Arguably, the trend may have reached its acme so far in the major Helm Identification Guide *Gulls of Europe, Asia and North America* by Klaus Malling Olsen and Hans Larsson.

17 : Camera obscura image

1826

A simple box with a hole in one end to let in light and a flat surface or screen at the other, where a colour image of the box's surroundings is projected upside down, some form of camera obscura has been known since around 2,400 BP, when it was mentioned in the surviving writings of the Chinese philosopher and founder of Mohism, Mozi (aka Mo Tzu). It is also mentioned not long after in a work by Aristotle (see pages 18–19).

By the 16th century, primitive lenses were being added to the entry hole, and they are believed to have been used as a drawing aid by Dutch painters including Vermeer. However, the projection of such images onto a light-sensitive surface resulted in the first permanent imprint of an image, when French scientist Joseph Nicéphore Niépce captured *View from the Window at Le Gras* on a bitumen-coated plate in 1826, though other processes like photogravure and lithography had been experimented with just a few years earlier.

Niépce formed a research partnership with Louis Daguerre, but it was not until after the former had died in 1833 that Daguerre managed to develop the first true photographic technique, which he termed, naturally, the daguerreotype. This technique involved making a true-life oriented or positive image on a silver-coated copper plate, but due to the lengthy exposure needed to obtain an image, the subjects were largely portraits or still lifes.

The development of wider lenses and refinements in the chemistry used kept shortening the exposure time, and the Dubroni camera of 1864, using the collodion wet plate process, enabled photographers to prepare their own plates inside the camera itself. Plate cameras into the early 20th century still took the form of large varnished boxes familiar from silent movies, more like items of furniture than the portable cameras we have taken for granted since the period between the two world wars.

However, these somewhat large and impractical cameras were also used for bird photography by the late 19th century, and have provided an invaluable record of what some relatively recently extinct species actually looked like in life, including captive Passenger Pigeons taken in 1896 and 1898, and the now-extinct endemic Laughing Owl from New Zealand, which was possibly photographed as early as 1889.

The fuzzy but identifiable *View from the Window at Le Gras* (above left, 1826) was the first image actually captured by a camera obscura. Plate cameras (above right) were good enough for Henry Charles Clarke Wright to preserve the appearance in life of the now-extinct Laughing Owl from New Zealand (top).

18 : Pig bristle paintbrushes

1827

While modern bird artists usually concentrate on their creative skills, perhaps combining this with a bit of birding or hobbyist natural history, for a good part of the 19th and early 20th centuries they were much more polymathic. The great bird artists of the Age of Exploration combined considerable abilities as scientists and adventurers, along with their creative capabilities.

In Britain, John Gould broke new ground in accuracy of rendition with his vibrant illustrations of Darwin's *Beagle* specimens (see pages 54–55), while in North America the ambitious and dashing John James Audubon made scientific, exploration and artistic history.

At 18, being of fighting age, Audubon first entered the United States in 1803 on a false passport to avoid the Napoleonic Wars, but immediately contracted yellow fever on arrival in New York city. Placed with quakers and nursed back to health, he travelled to his family's large homestead near Valley Forge, where he spent virtually every waking moment hunting, fishing, playing music and – significantly – drawing.

He quickly learnt a birder's field skills, and knew that understanding weather and habitat was the key to finding and identifying birds. Avoiding a potential career in a family mining business, Audubon began to study birds almost full time. He trapped local Eastern Phoebes, tied coloured cotton threads to their legs and was able to prove that they returned to their natal site every year, after migration; in essence, he thus invented bird ringing (see pages 82–83).

Frustrated by the lack of realism seen in other artists' depictions of America's birds, he determined to paint them true to life. Like many well-off naturalists of his day, he had a large collection of natural objects and taught himself taxidermy and other forms of specimen preparation. The sale of a business venture then enabled Audubon to pursue his dream of painting the entire avifauna of North America full-time.

Supplementing his income by giving drawing lessons, he travelled across the continent and had soon amassed enough drawings and paintings to consider printing them as a book. Taking a portfolio of around 300 pictures, he sailed to England and raised enough money to publish his classic major work, *The Birds of America* (1827-1838).

His innovatory methods of creating the

Artists like Audubon would have used handmade pig bristle brushes to capture the fine details of birds such as the Roseate Spoonbill featured in *The Birds of America*.

detailed and naturalistic paintings frequently involved 15-hour days preparing, posing and drawing his often self-collected specimens in scenes inspired by their natural habitat. Working in layered watercolour, chalk, pastels and gouache, he drew them all life-size, though he somewhat undermined the effect by contorting larger species to fit the standard paper sizes. However stylised and dramatic he made the scenes, the birds were always accurately drawn. Like most artists of his time, he also used handmade brushes of pig bristles and made his own pigments; while inconvenient, this meant he could replenish materials when travelling.

Such was the reach of his reputation after *The Birds of America* was published that his name became synonymous with wild birds in the USA, and America's national bird conservation organisation the National Audubon Society was named in his honour – its founder, George Grinnell, was profoundly inspired by reading Audubon's *Ornithological Biography* (1839), another major work.

Perhaps the most notable bird artist in Britain in the 19th century, Archibald Thorburn, also worked in a detailed and naturalistic fashion, creating his best-known works around the turn of the 20th century, including Christmas cards for the RSPB from 1899 onwards. Refusing to use anything other than natural light, Thorburn produced works that are still rated by modern bird illustrators as perhaps the most accurate renderings of British birds, though Gould was the undisputed prior painter of foreign birds.

19 : Raven cage

1829

Menageries — collections of live wild animals for display — have been known for at least 5,500 years, with remains of the most ancient (so far) unearthed at Hierakonpolis, Egypt, in 2009. They mostly featured dramatic large mammals, but Ostrich was certainly present in the 18th century in the Royal Menagerie at the Tower of London, where one died swallowing nails in 1791, due to the prevalent belief that the species could digest metal. The menagerie was first opened to the public during the reign of Elizabeth I in the 16th century.

Aviaries, or flight cages, are large mesh or net enclosures or captive areas where birds can fly relatively freely, often with some approximation of natural habitat or at least perches and feeding areas assembled within. These structures were most probably first used to display birds in the 19th century, and the Raven Cage in London Zoo is widely viewed to be one of the first, dating from 1829. This was still not much more than a very big cage, and the first large aviary in a zoo was at Rotterdam Zoo in 1880.

Very large aviaries were developed in several American institutions in the early 20th century, and the 1904 World's Fair Flight Cage in St Louis Zoo became the largest ever bird cage; it still exists today. The World's Fair organisers paid $3,500 for the cage, leaving them with insufficient money to populate it with birds; locals had to donate a few owls, Mandarin Ducks and Canada Geese.

It occurred to zoo owners that some aviaries were getting large enough for the public to actually walk among the birds. The Antwerp Zoo cage system was developed in 1948, with the public walkway kept dark while the birds were well-lit, the latter avoiding the path due to it being 'night' there. The 1960s saw several walk-in aviaries being built, with Frankfurt Zoo developing first its Bird Thicket in 1963 — 10 connected aviaries featuring different habitats — and then the Bird Halls, with a walk-through simulation of a tropical rainforest among other buildings. The following year, the ever-innovative London Zoo opened the huge Snowdon Aviary, still in use today.

Frankfurt's expansive offering was trumped by New York's Bronx Zoo with its two-storey World of Birds exhibit, featuring 25 one-way walk-through habitats, then the Henry Doorly Zoo in Nebraska, USA, with its Simmons Aviary opening in 1983 with more than 500 birds from all parts of the globe. The largest

Decimus Burton was London Zoo's official
architect from 1826 to 1841, and his
so-called 'Raven Cage' was actually first
built to house a pair of King Vultures.

aviary in the world is Birds of Eden,
Plettenburg Bay, South Africa, which opened
for business in 2005, and extends over
21,761m^2, holding about 3,000 individuals of
some 200 bird species.

While many conservationists and birders are
ambivalent about exotic birds being held in
cages, there can be no doubt that many such
collections are useful for highly sensitive
species preservation projects. Bird collections
have been largely responsible for the continued
survival of species once near extinction, like
Hawaiian Goose and Bali Starling, and have
been instrumental in developing the captive
breeding projects that keep birds like these out
of the annals of the lost.

20 : HMS *Beagle*

1831

What would birding be without the theory of evolution? A lot easier but not as engrossing, and for the eternal diversion of relationships and 'lumps' and 'splits' between species, above all we have Charles Darwin to thank.

Arguably, Darwin would not have come to his still radical-to-some conclusions without the opportunity to become ship's naturalist on ex-Royal Navy 'brig-sloop' HMS *Beagle*. The ship undertook three worldwide expeditions between 1825 and 1843, the first and second mostly under the captainship of Flag Lieutenant Robert Fitzroy. HMS *Beagle* set sail from Plymouth in October 1831 with Darwin on board, for its second voyage, on which it would survey much of South America, returning famously via the Galápagos Islands, then New Zealand and Australia, finally reaching Cornwall in October 1836.

The geological surveys and natural history observations from the expedition took Darwin almost 23 years to digest. His resulting work, *On The Origin of Species*, went on sale in November 1859. While the book covered a breathtaking range of natural history subjects, it was immediately applicable to ornithology. Long

before publication, John Gould (see pages 54–55) had pointed out in 1837 that Darwin's specimen of a rhea from the South American mainland was different to the known species, and that finches and mockingbirds found on the Galápagos differed from island to island.

The voyage itself took place after the 'Age of Exploration', as historians have dubbed the period between the 15th and 17th centuries, and most of the world's major trade routes had by then been established, with colonial stop-overs possible on many coasts during the voyage. The main purpose of HMS *Beagle*'s voyage was actually to undertake hydrographic surveys of the coast of South America, to produce sea charts for the military and the merchant navy. The then 22-year-old Charles Darwin was accepted onto the expedition as the ship's geologist, and had to pay his own way. He already had a gift for theorising, partly inspired by the relative practical inadequacy of the geological textbooks of the time, which would give him a temporal context for his imaginings of how animals and plants changed over time.

His theory has become more unassailable

Conrad Martens, official artist of the second voyage of *HMS Beagle*
(1831–1836), depicted the ship in watercolours in his painting *Mount
Sarmiento, Tierra del Fuego* (above) as it was moored on this
southernmost coast of South America. Inland, Darwin collected
specimens of an unknown ratite, later to be named Darwin's Rhea (top).

over the years, and is now virtually universally accepted as a natural law in biology. In ornithology, it enables the understanding of the ancestral relationships between species, to draw up rational classifications and sort birds into the genera, species and subspecies that birders love to identify in a field context. Once understood, it is viewed by most as an enrichment of the appreciation of the variation, and overwhelming variety, of birds.

21 : Wildlife garden

c. 1835

Basic awareness of ecology, the study of the interconnection of all living things, probably entered popular consciousness en masse in the 1950s and 1960s, and was propagated and spread by the progressively eco-conscious television programmes of the 1970s onwards. However, ecology itself has a longer history – and in the basic back-yard representation of the wildlife garden, dates back to about 1835.

A semblance of ecological thought had existed for many centuries before that, since at least the time of Aristotle's writings (see pages 18-19), but it was during the exploratory expansion of the 19th century that disciplined investigation of life's interactions began to increase. Such knowledge was also tied in to agricultural innovations and the Park Grass Experiment, where the effects of different fertilisers on the yield of hayfields began to be studied in 1856 at Rothamsted Experimental Station, Hertfordshire. Experiments at the site continue today, providing an invaluable continuum of environmental knowledge on pollution, the effects of climate change and even the selective influence of these factors on local evolutionary change.

Alfred Russel Wallace proposed his biogeographical zones (see pages 64-65) fully aware that each biota was interdependent, and many authors in the mid-1800s were using the concepts in their research and writings, including Darwin. The term ecology was first used by Ernst Haeckel in 1866.

With the term 'ecosystem', Arthur Tansley provided a catch-all name for the interactions of living things and their environment, and since then most people have understood – intuitively or in fact – that organisms rely on each other for survival and to control or expand their populations. Such awareness has extended right into the life of the individual, and a sizeable proportion of the public appreciate their garden birds and know that providing food and habitat for them is essential to maintain their presence around our properties and towns.

This awareness and appreciation probably owes its prevalence to the introduction of simple ecological concepts into the classroom and into front rooms via television wildlife documentaries. Prime time and post-school shows like *Animal Magic* featured 'how to make a wildlife garden' segments, and many watched Phil Drabble's efforts to design his own nature reserve, documented in *Design for a Wilderness*; droves of people were inspired to make room

A wildlife garden helps to compensate for the disappearance of habitat and invertebrate food from the modern urban environment. The above garden includes native trees and hedges for displaying and nesting birds, and a pond where birds can bathe and drink.

for nature in their own gardens, or at least retire to the countryside.

The British have had a long and enduring relationship with their gardens and many a nascent birder has first been hooked on the hobby by the youthful sighting of a more unusual bird table visitor or berry bush denizen, like Reed Bunting or Redwing.

Many modern private garden designers and landscapers offer wildlife-friendly options,

encouraging the patchy pockets of habitat that provide dispersal corridors between more wild or extensive sites, and along with railway embankments, prevent isolated 'islands' of species from becoming too inbred and enable the expansion of many familiar species' ranges. With urban and suburban green spaces being ever-encroached upon by cash-strapped councils and speculative developers, gardens now need to be 'wilded' even more than before.

22 : Gould's paintings of Darwin's finches and mockingbirds

1838

Perhaps the most well-known example of modern day evolution in action is the group of seed-eating tanagers usually referred to as Darwin's finches, all of which evolved from a single grassquit species within the last two million years.

Darwin collected many bird specimens from the Galápagos Islands, Ecuador, during the second voyage of HMS *Beagle* (1831-1836), and gave the whole lot to John Gould (1804-1881), taxidermist, ornithologist and bird artist in the museum at the Zoological Society of London, for identification and classification (see pages 48-49). Gould quickly realised that the finches were all closely related, even though Darwin had suggested that they were a mixed bag of New World blackbirds, a wren, 'gross-bills' and finches. He was also able to point out that Darwin's mockingbirds were also separate species and different from, but closely related to, a mainland South American form.

Darwin had even neglected to label the birds with the names of the islands where they were collected, and so labelled specimens kept by others on the expedition had to be recalled. Once the specimens had been assigned to collection sites, it became apparent that all were restricted to particular islands, despite their often obvious affinities. This realisation was a big step towards Darwin's conception of evolution by natural selection.

Gould painstakingly drew and painted these exotic but monochrome species in his detailed and naturalistic style, and published them between 1838 and 1842 in a part-work entitled *The Zoology of the Voyage of H.M.S. Beagle Under the Command of Captain Fitzroy, R.N., during the Years 1832 to 1836*. He soon went on to author and illustrate comprehensive and copiously illustrated works on the avifaunas of other countries. He published *A Century of Birds from the Himalaya Mountain* (1831-1832), a 20-part series with 80 colour plates, and perhaps his biggest innovation from a modern birder's point of view, the five-volume *The Birds of Europe* (1837) which features his own lithographic work hand-coloured by Edward Lear and Gould's wife, Elizabeth.

Gould's true-to-life renditions of plants and birds, and the compilation of his work into regional volumes, helped form a tradition of naturalistic bird art that still informs modern monographs and field guides, and can be seen in the work of today's foremost avian illustrators such as Ian Lewington, Killian Mullarney and Lars Jonsson, among a great many others.

Gould's illustration of San Cristóbal Mockingbird from his
The Zoology of the Voyage of HMS Beagle Part III: Birds.
He was the first to realise that many of Darwin's specimens
from different islands were related to each other, but it took
the collector himself to realise and understand why.

23 : Policeman's notebook

1840

All aspects of the hobby of birding revolve around the ability to recognise and identify different species, and when the observations are to be used as ornithological data then the accuracy of this is even more imperative.

For as long as people have observed birds, the correct identification of an unknown individual bird has hinged on the details of field notes entered into a pocket notebook. The traditional medium to record notes on habitat, feeding, plumage, behaviour, call, song and numbers has often been the policeman's notebook, a vertically opening black book measuring around 105x75mm, with a built-in elastic band to mark the page where the last entry was made, and containing around 80 to 100 leaves of ruled paper. Sometimes a short pencil will fit into the spine or a side flap of the book, and the back at least is usually made of stiff card.

The official 'PNB' is governed by strict guidelines, as evidence noted in the book must be admissible in court, but its history and design has meant that it is cheap, handy and practical, lending itself to rapid use in the field.

The first known standardised police notebook is documented in 1840, 11 years after the founding of the Metropolitan Police. Until that time, pads resembling jotters were generally used, and many police forces did not fall into line before the early 20th century. However, the convenience of the official notebook is such that it has survived almost unchanged to the present day.

While police officers are obliged to use standard-issue equipment, there is no law that says a birder must do so, and many different notebook styles are used, with different observers favouring side- or top-opening books, plain, ruled or graph paper and ring or perfect binding. Notebooks are now designed specifically for the birding market, and feature waterproof covers and/or paper, while waterproof pens and pencils are cheap and commonly available.

Notes may also be kept according to personal style, from straightforward, as-it-happens scrawling to carefully tabulated and itemised counts and measurements. Many keep their records for purely personal reasons, but with the advent of the concept of 'citizen science', more and more birders are keeping meticulous and accurate records; these can be sent in to bird recorders or entered online via survey schemes such as the Cornell Lab of

Still used by many birders, the policeman's notebook fits perfectly into a pocket and is just the right size to draw field sketches and make notes.

Ornithology eBird and the British Trust for Ornithology's BirdTrack. These online databases keep track of bird movements, arrival and departure dates, distributions and populations for the greater good of science and conservation. They are a sure way of making observations 'count' for more than just personal interest.

Traditionally, birders have often entered their notes into a journal or bird diary, much in the tradition of Gilbert White (see pages 34–35), keeping their records in a legible form and adding further sketches and annotations to make sense of what they had seen. Since the end of the 20th century, software packages have begun to be used to keep account of what a birder has seen, and these have become increasingly more sophisticated; packages now hold trip and site records, including checklists in various taxonomies, have photographs and sound recordings for reference, and cross-referencing capability. Electronic records are now often stored online, and already field observations can be immediately entered into online databases and quickly processed and analysed.

Whatever their purpose, virtually all birders take and keep notes, and it is an important part of what is ultimately an observational and self-educational pastime.

24 : Bird table

c. 1850

While there is little written history of bird feeding, and certainly few remaining antique bird feeders, the first intentional provision of food specifically for wild birds appears to have been by the 6th century monk Saint Serf of Fife, Scotland, who, when not performing legendary miracles, was said to have tamed a Robin by feeding it, according to James Fisher in *The Shell Bird Book* (1966).

Although the first prototype bird table design appeared in about 1850, the act of deliberate bird feeding largely disappeared from the historical record until 1890, when newspapers encouraged people to help birds survive that year's harsh winter by putting out scraps in their gardens. The practice continued henceforth after this apparently pivotal moment, and was already considered a popular pastime in Britain before the First World War. It rapidly spread around the globe, with everything from hummingbirds in Trinidad to weavers in The Gambia and honeycreepers in Australia being encouraged to visit bird tables and suspended feeders.

Tables and feeders range in design from the baroque to the rustic, and from the rococo to the prosaic. Simple, practical designs have been published in popular birdwatching and ornithological books since at least the 1940s, with even the most primitive of carpentry skills being catered for. Plain seed mixes have now become more targeted with the seed of Nyjer (a trademarked species of Ethiopian daisy) incorporated for small finches and fat and suet recipes have also been prevalent since at least the 1960s.

There is no doubt that providing food for wild birds saves avian lives in hard weather, and can help supplement the nutrient and energy intakes of breeding birds. Bird feeding has also been shown to affect the very evolution of garden bird species, as in the case of Blackcaps from Germany. These insectivorous and frugivorous warblers migrate partly to Britain in winter and have thinner bills to get at suet in bird feeders; the more southern and slightly thicker-billed population migrates to Spain, where they eat ripe olives and other fruits. Conversely, bird feeding has also been implicated in reductions in survival in Blue Tit.

The presence of birds near houses and gardens, especially in urban environments, can be the only real contact with nature that some people have, and is important for keeping that one fragile thread intact – a connection healthy for both spirit and for conservation.

Bird tables not only bring birds near to the
observer or garden owner, but also provide
a valuable service in feeding birds in times
of austerity, particularly in winter.

25 : First issue of *The Ibis*

1859

While ornithology had been developing in semi-isolation among general biologists, its popularity and rapid development required both organisation and a repository for the latest research.

Britain was the first country to do this when the British Ornithologists' Union (BOU) was formed in 1858, producing the first issue of its journal *The Ibis*, subtitled the *International Journal of Avian Science*, the following year. The union itself was formed by a coterie of distinguished scientists including Henry Tristram (for whom Tristram's Warbler was named), and its presidents have included many luminaries of British ornithology, some of them commemorated in the scientific names of assorted species. The BOU began maintaining a list of British birds almost immediately, as well as helping to raise money to fund its own research.

There was no officially scrutinised and moderated British list until 1920 when, despite no clear public announcement over their veracity at the time, widespread doubts over the faking of the specimens which were to become known as the 'Hastings rarities' resulted in the formation of the BOU's Records Committee (BOURC).

America followed, and the American Ornithologists' Union coalesced in 1883, creating the foundations for bird study and conservation there. It, too, began to publish its own journal, *The Auk*, and a list, *The AOU Check-list of North American Birds*. Both the AOU and BOU lists provide the standard reference for accepted occurrences and taxonomy, as well as the official English and scientific names for North America and Britain.

Though with significant academic input, these organisations can both lay claim to the gradual popularisation of studying and watching birds for its own sake, and innovations in optics design meant that by 1889, an American field guide with a practical angle was available: *Birds Through an Opera Glass* by Florence Bailey. In 1901, the term 'birdwatching' was coined by Edmund Selous in an eponymous volume.

With parallel development of conservation organisations on both sides of the Atlantic in the Audubon Society and the RSPB, members of the public interested in birds began to turn against the 'shoot 'em and see' methods of bird identification, adopting instead the scientific community's observational tactics.

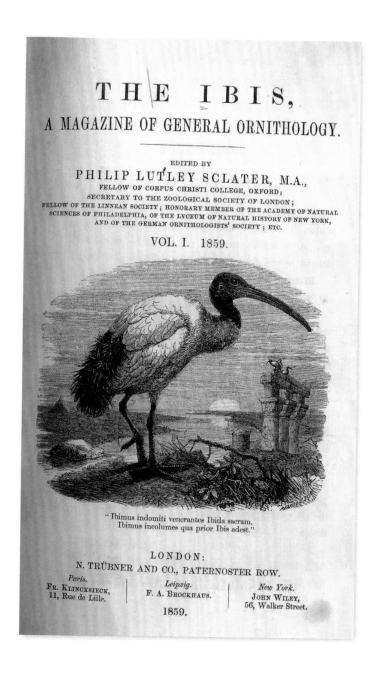

THE IBIS,

A MAGAZINE OF GENERAL ORNITHOLOGY.

EDITED BY
PHILIP LUTLEY SCLATER, M.A.,
FELLOW OF CORPUS CHRISTI COLLEGE, OXFORD;
SECRETARY TO THE ZOOLOGICAL SOCIETY OF LONDON;
FELLOW OF THE LINNEAN SOCIETY; HONORARY MEMBER OF THE ACADEMY OF NATURAL
SCIENCES OF PHILADELPHIA, OF THE LYCEUM OF NATURAL HISTORY OF NEW YORK,
AND OF THE GERMAN ORNITHOLOGISTS' SOCIETY; ETC.

VOL. I. 1859.

"Ibimus indomiti venerantes Ibida sacram,
Ibimus incolumes qua prior Ibis adest."

LONDON:
N. TRÜBNER AND CO., PATERNOSTER ROW.

Paris.
FR. KLINCKSIECK,
11, Rue de Lille.

Leipzig.
F. A. BROCKHAUS.

New York.
JOHN WILEY,
56, Walker Street.

1859.

First published in 1859, The Ibis is still one of the foremost ornithological journals in the world, though it has been superseded by British Birds and the popular monthlies as far as providing information to birders goes.

26 : *Archaeopteryx* specimen

1861

After the publication of Charles Darwin's *On The Origin of Species by Means of Natural Selection, or the Preservation of Favoured Races in the Struggle for Life* in 1859, both the public and the scientific establishment were keen to see fossil evidence of forms intermediate between the different kinds of animal that we see today, in particular the major groups; this would surely be proof of Darwin's then contentious big idea.

Almost immediately, a feather unearthed in a limestone quarry near Solnhofen, Germany, in 1860 whetted the appetites of those seeking ancestral birds, though a solitary feather merely indicated the presence of bird-like animals in the late Jurassic period (about 150 million years ago). However, the discovery the following year of a headless but otherwise near-complete skeleton of what appeared to be a creature halfway between true birds and theropod dinosaurs caused a storm.

The nature of the fine-grained limestone deposits of the Solnhofen area meant that they were the first extensively exploited deposits of the plattenkalk, used widely for lithography, a printing method involving etched images applied to an oiled layer on the surface of the stone. The super-fine grain of the stone enables extremely fine preservation of the fauna of the area in Jurassic times, including remarkable details of feathers.

The first confirmed specimen of the *Urvogel* (meaning 'original bird') was given in lieu of a payment to a local doctor, Karl Häberlein, who then sold it to the London Natural History Museum for £700, this fossil becoming known as the 'London specimen'. Eleven *Archaeopteryx* specimens have now been unearthed, each having been given its own species name at some time, though they are usually lumped under the name *Archaeopteryx lithographica*, originally given to the first (possibly unrelated) feather.

However, in modern terms it is quite possible that all are separate species, in much the same way as several species of thrush might occupy the same habitats at certain times of year and potentially be preserved, and also that these are likely to have evolved somewhat in the geologically short period of just a few million years.

All specimens share almost all their physical features, and are essentially small theropod dinosaurs to go by their toothed jaws, three-fingered hands, feathers (it is now known that feathers were common in dinosaurs), a killing claw on the second toe, and a long, bony tail. However, some avian features are obvious: long, strong flight and tail feathers, and a wishbone, for instance.

The feathers are key: *Archaeopteryx* had asymmetrical, vaned flight feathers very similar to modern birds, indicating that it could generate lift and may have possessed controlled flight capability, though many think

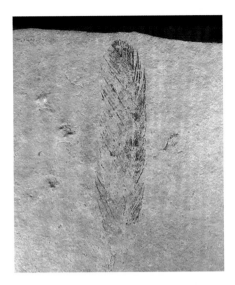
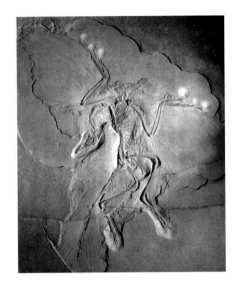

First described in 1861 from a single (possibly unrelated) feather dug up the previous year, *Archaeopteryx* is now known from 11 almost complete fossils, including the 'Berlin specimen' (above right), unearthed in 1874 or 1875, which has revealed the most details of its body and leg feathering.

that it was a glider rather than flyer, owing to its flat rather than keeled sternum. Close examination of the later 'Berlin specimen' showed it to have had 'trousers' — upper leg feathers like some birds of prey — and contour feathers on the body. Analysis of the London specimen's braincase indicated the proportionately large brain needed for flight.

How big were these beasts? The different specimens vary from the size of Azure-winged Magpie up to Roadrunner, and there are indications that they led a partially terrestrial existence like the latter species, though lifestyle is still the subject of fierce debate. We do know from preserved pigment cells in some of the wing feathers that *Archaeopteryx* had some black in its plumage, consistent with many modern

birds which use the structural properties of melanin to strengthen their wing feathers. The growth rings in its bones indicate diurnal activity, and also that it was a fairly slow-growing species, taking up to three years to reach full size.

Archaeopteryx's fairly arid, subtropical lagoon habitat had low-growing, shrubby vegetation, and like many modern forms it had a habitat-specific range and some variation in size and shape between the different 'species' which may even have required some field skill to tell apart, had they been truly contemporary.

We can only guess at that, but *A. lithographica*'s finely preserved detail means that its status as an intermediate between dinosaurs and modern birds is firmly written in stone.

27 : Wallace's map of the Earth's biogeographical regions

1876

Birders love lists, and are particularly fond of keeping lists for geographical areas, whether on a local or global scale. For those able to travel beyond the borders of their own countries, lists are usually kept on the basis of the zoogeographical zones of the world.

These zones are generally accepted by biologists as logical and accurate ways of physically dividing the Earth's animals and plants into separate geographical and evolutionary lineages and histories. More precisely, those regions can be defined by their biotas, which in turn reflect the geological and spatial separation of those regions.

Alfred Russel Wallace (1823-1913) is perhaps best known as biology's 'nearly man' – he came up with his own theory of evolution simultaneously with Charles Darwin, and it was Wallace's determination to publish his work that forced Darwin into publicly revealing what popular history sometimes forgets was actually more of a joint presentation of both scientists' work. Wallace independently came up with the idea of natural selection as a driver of evolution, and remained a die-hard defender of this idea, but was also forward-thinking enough to consider environmental influences as important as, or even more so, than the inter- and intra-species competition that Darwin cited.

Encouraged by contemporaries including Darwin, Wallace also began his life's research into the distribution of the various types of animal around the globe, getting into his stride in 1874 after more accurate taxonomies had been devised. Factoring in the contemporary belief in land bridges (this was before the continents were known to drift on their crustal plates), as well as glaciation, geographical barriers like oceans and mountains, and the vegetation zones of the planet, he was able to map the major biotas of the Earth by summarising the known distributions of genera and families of animals, the majority of which had already been discovered by the time he was writing.

The resulting book, *The Geographical Distribution of Animals* (1876), would remain the standard text until at least the Second World War, and put names to six of the eight biogeographical realms (also termed ecozones in modern publications) which are in use today: Nearctic (most of North America into Mexico); Neotropic (essentially Central and South America and the Caribbean); Palearctic (Europe, North Africa, the Middle East and

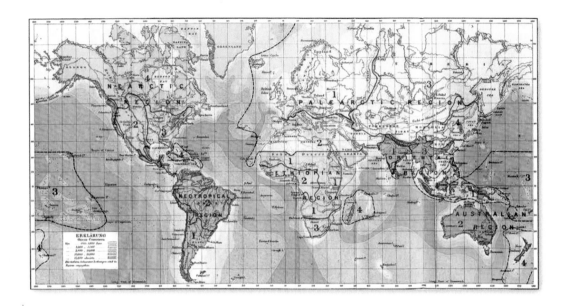

Wallace's early map of the zoogeographical zones of the Earth has changed little in the interim, and the regions described still assist in understanding how and why animals are distributed around the planet in the way they are. They also help birders set limits to their listing.

Asia north of the Himalayas); Ethiopian (now known as Afrotropic, covering sub-Saharan Africa and Madagascar); Oriental (or Indomalayan, covering the Indian subcontinent and South-East Asia); and Australian (Australia, New Guinea and associated islands). The two additional realms are Antarctica and Oceania. Each of these has a distinct fauna and flora – and avifauna – with many more endemic forms than cosmopolitan.

With refinements, these zones remain pretty much intact today, and one of the greatest refinements was named after the great man himself: Wallace's Line. On his extensive travels in Indonesia, he noticed a clear transition between the faunas of Australia and Asia across the distance of the Lombok Strait

between the islands of Lombok and Bali, only 35 miles apart at their closest. This deep water barrier extends north between Sulawesi and Borneo, and remains a clear faunal divider along its whole length. We now know that the barrier remained intact even when glaciation was at its height, greatly increasing the area of the adjacent land masses.

The Palearctic region is commonly separated into Western and Eastern sub-regions, using the Ural Mountains as the dividing line in tune with the principles laid down by Wallace almost a century and a half before. In this way, his contributions to zoology and evolutionary theory are unwittingly commemorated when every birder 'ticks off' a new species on their 'West Pal' list.

28 : Microphone

1877

Much emphasis is placed on bird song as a means by which we can identify different species (and, indeed, how they identify themselves), and central to our understanding of avian vocalisations is the ability to record the sounds birds make. Cue the microphone.

The first 'mic' was the subject of bitter argument and courtroom battle as American inventors Thomas Edison and Emile Berliner registered patents for the first such carbon prototypes in 1877. These small devices with a visual resemblance to buttons converted sound to electrical charge by using the pressure on carbon granules between two metal plates to transform sound waves to a current. Edison and Berliner would be racing neck-and-neck for much of the early history of recorded sound.

However, listening to recorded sound also necessitated a medium for its preservation. Though sound had first been represented visually by the phonautograph in 1857, Edison was able to manufacture the first phonograph in 1878, just a year after the first microphone. It consisted of a wax, foil or lead cylinder onto which a stylus engraved grooves, according to changes in air pressure created by the original sound waves. Amplification of the resulting grooves could produce a playback of the original sounds, a process that still seems slightly magical no matter to what depth it is explained.

This aura of inexplicability certainly piqued public interest and fuelled the ensuing race, and Berliner was able to trump Edison with the gramophone, using a similar technique to produce audio from grooves on a flat disc. This had the advantage of being easily reproduced commercially and cheaply, by impressing the grooves onto a negative master which then imprinted them on a plate or disc made of shellac, a resin secreted by a scale insect from India and South-East Asia. Through the first half of the 20th century, countless discs of this material were sold, including many recordings of bird song.

Edison's phonographs went into commercial production almost immediately, and one purchased at the Leipzig Fair in Germany in 1889 was given as a present to eight-year-old Ludwig Koch, with dramatic results (see pages 70-71).

VOICI LE PREMIER PHONOGRAPHE D'EDISON. IL ETAIT LOIN DES APPAREILS D'AUJOURD'HUI

NOTRE photographie représente le premier phonographe inventé par Edison en 1877.

L'appareil représenté ci-contre se compose essentiellement d'un cylindre recouvert d'un manchon de cire durcie dont l'axe tourne dans deux paliers. Une manivelle, fixée à l'une des extrémités de l'axe, commande la rotation du cylindre; l'autre extrémité est munie d'un volant lourd qui favorise l'uniformité du mouvement de rotation communiqué par la manivelle. Le cylindre se déplace de gauche à droite (droite à gauche si l'on regarde la gravure) devant le diaphragme. Ce dernier est constitué par une membrane métallique munie d'une aiguille d'ivoire. L'embouchure, ou pavillon, est formée par une sorte de cornet acoustique renversé dont la plus petite ouverture est fermée par le diaphragme.

Aujourd'hui, le manchon de cire durcie a fait place au disque, infiniment moins encombrant, moins altérable et moins fragile. La pointe du stylet, en acier trempé dans les appareils modestes, est un saphir dans les phonographes de luxe; le pavillon est souvent supprimé et remplacé par une caisse à résonance. Enfin, dans les grands appareils, la rotation du disque se fait à l'aide d'un moteur électrique pourvu d'un régulateur et dans les phonographes ordinaires au moyen d'un mécanisme d'horlogerie que l'on remonte après chaque audition.

LE PREMIER PHONOGRAPHE
INVENTÉ PAR LE CÉLÈBRE INGÉNIEUR AMÉRICAIN ÉDISON

Soon after its invention in 1878 the Edison phonograph (above) was on sale in most western countries, producing recorded sound from a grooved wax cylinder. The top image shows the interior of a later Ericsson carbon microphone.

29 : Meinertzhagen's Forest Owlet specimen

1880

The rediscovery of the Forest Owlet in India in 1997 was greeted with widespread delight. This small diurnal owl of the Maharashtra region had previously been known from only seven specimens, including four collected in the same region by J Davidson between 1880 and 1883, and a last specimen claimed by Colonel Richard Meinertzhagen to have been collected in Gujarat, more than 500 miles away, just over 30 years later.

As some of Meinertzhagen's specimens had been exposed as having been stolen and fraudulently relabelled, the scientists who rediscovered the owlet painstakingly examined his stuffed Forest Owlet which was housed in the Natural History Museum, Tring.

X-rays determined that the preparation of all the examples was identical, and it was also revealed that a fifth Davidson specimen had existed but was now missing. Meinertzhagen wasn't in that region of India at the time he said he collected the bird, and never published anything on this extremely rare species. The specimen had almost certainly been stolen and added to the colonel's own personal collection of 20,000 prepared bird skins.

In any hobby – or indeed in science – there are ways to profit. They can be financial, or involve gaining respect, giving the impression of authoritativeness or even feeling a sense of superiority over others. The science of ornithology and the pastime of birding have both always had room for discovery and earning plaudits. In tandem with the rise of private and museum collections of exotica came the ability to 'pull the wool' and profiteer.

Financial gain had the greatest influence from the 18th to the early 20th centuries, and in Britain this partly came from the desire of some wealthy collectors to possess the rarest British-caught specimens. Surprisingly, at the beginning of the 1700s, proof or assurance of the veracity of valuable specimens was far from common, and this enabled, for example, butterfly specimens to be passed off as 'new species' by the addition of ink or paint.

As brutally simple as such frauds appear, birds were initially harder to pass off as being genuinely caught in the British Isles. With exotic species being imported preserved in alcohol or as desiccated wings, heads and tails, it was difficult to defraud a potential customer. But after it was discovered that mixing salt with water could result in the ability to preserve specimens at temperatures well below freezing point and the transport of frozen food became common, fresh-looking specimens became easy to acquire in bulk.

By the late 19th century, the transport of frozen fish and poultry was taking place on an

The Forest Owlet was perhaps the most notorious specimen stolen by eminent ornithologist Richard Meinertzhagen, who threw doubt onto his life's work, much of which was probably sound, by his lack of discipline when it came to collecting bird specimens.

industrial scale. This was the likely background to the notorious Hastings Rarities scandal, in which the belated rejection of almost 600 records involving rare bird specimens took place after they were considered to be part of a conspiracy to make money by a local taxidermist called George Bristow, along with unknown or unnameable ornithologists and collectors, by importing foreign bird corpses in this manner. The number and location of the specimens made it highly unlikely that they were genuine, and it is damning that none of the other then numerous local taxidermists had anything like a similar selection of preserved birds for sale.

Self-aggrandisement can be an even greater motivator for deceit. This takes us full circle to Colonel Meinertzhagen, perhaps one of the most heroic ornithologists during the decline of the British Empire. Many of the tales of colonial derring-do on his part had, it later transpired, originated purely in the mind of the protagonist, who was also posthumously revealed to be an unpunished murderer, a thief and a cheat.

Through his career as collector, ornithologist, writer and vice-president of the BOU, he stole specimens from museums,

relabelled them as his own and took credit for new discoveries. When specimens in the Tring collection were analysed for their taxidermy style, dates and locations of collection, many were found to be inconsistent and unlikely.

Acquisitive, amoral and impatient, Meinertzhagen's self-indulgence has tainted the reputation and achievements of a man whose work was genuinely brilliant and ground-breaking (including discovering a genuine new species in Afghan Snowfinch). His dark double life has seen the posthumous undoing of most of his work.

With the recognition granted to the rarity finder in today's birding scene, it is unsurprising to find that fraud continues and, when suspected, lack of concrete evidence enables many to get away with it. The most notorious rare bird fraud in Britain in recent years involved the fifth national record of a Hermit Thrush from North America, purportedly from Chipping Ongar, Essex, in October 1994. It was accepted by the Rarities Committee despite damning circumstantial evidence, and eventually revealed as a hoax by the submitter of the record, who unmasked himself in a confessional article some years later in *Birdwatch* magazine.

30 : Photographic film

1885

The large plates used for photography in the late 19th century were somewhat impractical due to their size, weight, long exposure and other inconveniences of use. Despite these drawbacks, they were still used to a limited extent in nature photography, particularly as the quality of the glass in the plates was better than any other known transparent media.

But in 1885 a coating (or 'film') of cellulose nitrate backed with thin paper became the first flexible medium of continuous use, and was developed by George Eastman. Though highly flammable, the film layer could be rapidly exposed, and then peeled from its backing and mounted on glass to be used for printing. Despite the popular perception of early photographs being black-and-white or sepia-toned, colour photography using the three basic colours of red, green and blue was already shown to be possible by 1861, though the methods were cost-prohibitive and complex.

James Clark Maxwell was the man who first publicly demonstrated the techniques at the Royal Institution, London, in that year, using slides of a tartan ribbon taken through red, green and blue filters which, when projected together through each other in a lantern slide projector, gave an anaemic but fairly life-like representation of true colour.

The much shorter exposure needed to use the many forms of colour and black-and-white film which were rapidly and continuously developed through the late 19th century attracted the attentions of most serious photographers, including a pupil at Enfield Grammar School, Middlesex, named Oliver Pike. Pike had befriended a local photographer and amateur ornithologist called Reginald Badham Lodge, who was already specialising in bird photography by 1890 when the two met, and the young Pike began accompanying Lodge on his nature forays.

The mentorship between the two talented photographers yielded much fruit, and in 1895 they developed a trip-wire shutter release mechanism, a method still in refined use today to enable birds and other animals to trigger cameras. Lodge made a business from his techniques, but it was Pike who ran with the ideas, publishing a series of guides to bird photography, then adding bird cinematography to his curriculum vitae. His *Birdland* series of books and films helped popularise birdwatching as a hobby to its own ends (Lodge's participation in the hobby had involved substantial amounts of shooting).

James Clark Maxwell (top) used the red, green and blue filters of a tartan ribbon to produce almost lifelike colours, paving the way to the development of the first colour photographic film.

Birdland (1907) was Pike's first feature film and was shown to large and appreciative paying crowds in cinemas who were either keen to see the secrets of seabird colonies recorded by Pike and colleagues abseiling down the cliffs with cameras, or attracted by the sheer novelty of these innovative insights. The 100 cinematic prints of this title were followed by two popular sequels, and Pike continued to make natural history films for the cinema well into the 20th century, pioneering filming within nest boxes in *A Family of Great Tits* (1934) and committing the famous breeding habits of Common Cuckoo to celluloid.

His passion for birds was not just confined to photography and cinema, and he was also a vigorous campaigner against egg collecting and bird hunting, making him not just unusual for the time, but perhaps the first modern birding all-rounder.

31 : Egret plume hat

1886

The beauty of birds' plumage has always been obvious, but rapid human population growth after the Industrial Revolution, along with the attendant increase in disposable income, resulted in the expanding ranks of the well-off beginning to demand the plumes of exotic birds as adornments for fashionable hats.

In parallel with this, the world's armed forces had long been using Ostrich and egret feathers for ceremonial hats. As the demand for both fashionable and military millinery increased, many species of wild bird were exploited on an industrial scale, and the populations of several egret and bird-of-paradise species were seriously depleted for their ostentatious plumes.

In 1886, Frank Chapman, an ornithologist at the American Museum of Natural History, performed a 'Feathered Hat Census' on 700 women's hats that he saw on the streets of Manhattan, New York. He was able to identify 40 species of American wild bird — sometimes with their entire skins stuffed and pinned in place — the most numerous of which were Common Tern, Northern Bobwhite, Northern Flicker, Cedar Waxwing and Snow Bunting. Egrets were already too scarce and expensive to feature on street wear, but feather trim also featured on the classic fedora hat, worn by the century's more sharply dressed men.

By the early 20th century, one in every thousand Americans was employed in the trade and egret feathers were worth $80 per ounce wholesale — more than four times as much as the contemporary gold price — and many populations of Snowy Egret in particular were approaching wipe-out. So closely were these birds associated with the plume trade that the French term for egret, *l'aigrette*, remains the fashion industry's term for decorative feathers — or jewellery — placed prominently on headwear. The showy plumes, so effective at attracting avian mates, had perhaps achieved a similar purpose in higher society, too.

At the London Commercial Sales Rooms in 1902, the feathers of some 192,960 herons and egrets were auctioned, their plucked bodies left to rot and, as the plumes were usually collected at their breeding colonies, their chicks — numbering at least 400,000 — left to starve.

Such plunder of a finite and visible natural resource was quickly noticed, and protests about the decline of Great Crested Grebe — its downy feathers used as a fur substitute in ladies' fashion — and Kittiwake in Britain led to protective legislation in 1880. New Zealand's endemic Huia was declared extinct in 1907, and it is also believed that Great Auk was partly wiped out due to the use of its feathers as a substitute for Eider down, when that species in turn was over-exploited in North America.

In the United States, Snowy Egret was adopted as the symbol of the bird preservation

There is little doubt that egret plumes look striking on both birds and hats, but the demand from fashionable women and milliners in the late 19th century caused a dangerous plummet in the numbers of white heron species across North America and Europe.

movement, and the American Ornithologists' Union, formed in 1883, had its first campaign, along with the Audubon Society. Volunteers and seasonal wardens guarded large wading bird colonies in areas like Corkscrew Swamp, Florida, as early as 1912. The law was on their side – 1900 saw the passing of the Lacey Act, the first national conservation legislation in the USA, later expanded to prevent imports of foreign wildlife and specimens, speeding up the ending of the illegal plume trade in North America.

Almost in parallel, the Society for the Protection of Birds (see pages 80–81) was formed in Britain in 1889 to counter the increasing international trade in exotic plumage. Among its professed rules was "that Lady-Members shall refrain from wearing the feathers of any bird not killed for purposes of food, the Ostrich only excepted".

In fact the exploitation of seabirds for their feathers continued into the 20th century, but due to the lobbying of the early conservationists, the wearing of wild bird plumes became unfashionable by the beginning of the First World War, possibly due to a collapse in prices as the world's markets and tastes became more austere, as well as mounting public disapproval.

After several aristocrats began to support the society, it was given a Royal Charter in 1904, allowing it to use the prefix 'Royal'. Eventually, ethically farmed Ostrich plumes became the decoration of choice for ceremonial hats, sparing the lives of many real 'fashion victims'.

32 : Winchester shotgun

1887

Before good quality optics, the only way to get close to birds – unless you were St Francis of Assisi – was to shoot them.

Inevitably, this was usually performed for the purpose of hunting for sport or for the pot, and the history of ornithology is far more closely tied to the history of firearms than today's conservation-oriented birders might care to admit. Equally as inevitably, the corpses of such fascinating and beautiful creatures led to curiosity about their plumage differences, relationships and habits.

It could be argued that, for some at least, hunting skills gradually matured into pure field skills. Hunting was used to collect specimens for trophies, and amass curiosities from expeditions overseas and specimens for private collections. The invention of the shotgun enabled specimen collection to develop into a multi-national, multi-million pound trade, as well as the only accurate way of discovering and evaluating the variation and different plumages of each bird species.

Pre-19th century hunters tended to use less accurate 'fowling pieces', with internally smooth, long barrels able to carry lead shot or round bullets like musket balls. The development of smaller-bore barrels with

rifling – spiral grooves along the inside length of the barrel, giving spin to the projectiles to increase accuracy – created the shotgun, a term first recorded in 1776 to cover both rifled and unrifled guns using lead shot (though now generally only used for smooth-bored weapons). By the mid-1880s, big 'punt guns' – essentially 'shot cannons' mounted on boats – were being used for commercial wildfowling. But it was double-barrelled shotguns that gained overall precedence in hunting, collecting and indeed warfare, and they are still the weapon of preference today for some game hunting.

Pump-action shotguns, in which the grip is slid or pumped forward and backward to expel a used shot cartridge and push a fresh one into the chamber, became very popular in the late 19th century due to the speed in which rounds could be ejected and refreshed. With the Winchester's improved accuracy in particular, this meant that it could be used as a very efficient weapon.

Winchester repeaters were 'the guns that won the West', but the arms-maker's shotguns could easily be called the 'guns that over-hunted the west'. Precision was unnecessary to make the Passenger Pigeon extinct – the scatter

The 'gun that won the west' could also be said to have devastated its fauna, being instrumental in the extinction and near-extinction of several bird and mammal species.

of a Winchester's shot was able to bring down 50 at once from the birds' famous sky-darkening migrating flocks.

Despite this and the many other ecological tragedies of 'manifest destiny', hunting has a close and perhaps unique relationship with conservation in the USA that it doesn't have in Europe. American hunters were quick to realise that wildlife needed to be preserved if they were to keep enjoying their sport. Hunters, led by Theodore Roosevelt among others, pressurised government for regulations to be drawn up and enforced, and conservation clubs and societies were formed to lobby and pay for the protection of habitat, often with the express philosophy that the land and its wildlife belonged to all Americans.

Huntsmen are still one of the largest funders of conservation in the United States, through taxes on guns and ammunition, a fact that makes many conservationists understandably uneasy.

33 : Parabolic reflector

1888

A bird's vocalisations can often be a feeble and mobile sound source, and therefore very difficult to record even with modern equipment, let alone with the first impractical recording machines which used cylinders (see pages 78–79). Clearly, a method had to be found to gather sound waves and concentrate them towards a microphone, in order to amplify the signal so that it could be isolated more efficiently from ambient background noise.

This idea had already been in use in optical design since the first telescopes were developed in the 15th century, using mirrors to concentrate light beams, but it took a German physicist named Heinrich Hertz to adapt the concept for sound waves. The first parabolic reflectors, essentially concave dishes with a microphone or receiver placed in a central focal point to gather the collected sound waves, were actually developed for radio waves, and most of the innovations were achieved as this technology grew.

Shotgun microphones, which only collect sound from sources directly in front of them, are the microphones of choice for most field recordists, but they only pick up loud, close sounds well. Parabolic reflectors eliminate much of the extraneous noise that may be present in the field, while isolating a particular bird's song when pointing the device directly at the source, and amplifying and concentrating it; in effect, they are the audio equivalent of a telephoto lens on a camera. Stereo sound is difficult to achieve owing to the circular and limited catchment of a reflector, and an omni-directional microphone must usually be used. The largely high-pitched nature of bird sound means that they can be recorded relatively well by parabolic microphone set-ups, which usually have a poor bass frequency response.

The first known use of a parabolic microphone set-up for wildlife recording came some 44 years after the invention of the reflector itself. In 1932 Peter Paul Kellogg, a professor at Cornell University, New York, used a somewhat "crude, awkward, bulky 'dish'" to make a field recording of a singing Yellow-breasted Chat onto the soundtrack of a film, 'optical' recording having already become a standard medium at the college. He and his colleagues experimented with different weights, sizes, focal lengths and materials, and used theoretical data already published in physics papers two years previously to refine their techniques.

An early parabolic reflector being deployed in the
field by Eric Simms, one of the pioneers of
bird-sound recording in the 20th century.

Technological advancements like directional microphones have meant that the principles of parabolic recording techniques no longer require a large reflecting dish, but the demands of amateur practitioners at least mean they are still often used by wildlife sound recordists. Well-designed plastic reflectors have also been marketed for the emptier pocket, and can produce very good results. Reflectors, or microphone kits incorporating their principles, are still in constant use in wildlife film-making and sound recording.

34 : Wax cylinder

1889

The young Ludwig Koch's nascent birdwatching interest was enhanced when he was presented with an Edison phonograph and several wax cylinders. With this basic kit he was able to record the song of a caged White-rumped Shama, an Asian species. This recording still exists and is widely believed to be the first ever bird sound recording.

The wax cylinder was the first commercially available medium for recorded sound between 1888 and 1929, and it was for this format and not vinyl or shellac discs that the term 'record' was first coined. The medium survived quite well as it was the only method of both recording and playback, an advantage over disc systems which were for reproduction only. The music industry is sometimes said to have started with a craze for bird song recordings in the very late 19th century, and some cylinders were sold with small whistles for imitating some of the songs on the cylinders.

Dissatisfied with written notations of bird song, Koch became an ornithologist with a clear ambition to compile recordings of avian vocalisations into a 'sound book'. He eventually achieved this in 1935, with the publication – or release in music industry terms – of *Gefiederte Meistersänger*, or *Feathered Master Singers*, featuring recordings of 25 common species chosen for their interesting vocalisations and pressed into shellac, the medium of choice for music and sound recordings until the 1950s.

Koch's timing was a little out, and he fled from the Nazis, arriving in Britain in 1936 with very few recordings. His reputation had preceded him and he began recording the songs of British birds, abetted by Sir Julian Huxley and with helpful interest from the BBC. British ornithologist Max Nicholson had almost simultaneously been commissioned to write a book about bird song, and joined forces with Koch to release *Songs of Wild Birds* (1936) and *More Songs of Wild Birds* (1937) in quick succession, documenting the sounds of 36 British species in total over five double-sided 10" records.

Now that modern technology permits everyone to record bird song with minimal effort, most mobile phones featuring a microphone and digital recorder facility, achievements such as Koch's are often forgotten. At the time, it was a breakthrough which shifted the landscape of amateur ornithology, and allowed the listener to enjoy – and learn – the songs of the birds around them in the comfort of their own homes.

Wax cylinders were the first transportable and
commercially available method of hearing recorded
sound, and continued to be manufactured until 1929.

35 : RSPB membership card

1889

Possibly the greatest influence on both British conservation and birdwatching has been the nation's foremost specialist ornithological charity, the Royal Society for the Protection of Birds.

Fittingly, the organisation had its roots in an anti-exploitation campaign opposed to the use of wild birds' feathers in fashionable ladies' hats (see pages 72–73), and was started by Emily Williamson and Eliza Phillips in 1889, then without its 'Royal' prefix. Initially composed mainly of society women who, like its founders, were horrified by the cruelty, waste and destruction of the plume industry, the addition of notable ornithologists to its ranks both promoted this cause and enabled the society to expand its remit substantially and with authority.

Granted a Royal Charter in 1904, the then London-based society had already begun producing publications, a constitution and Christmas cards, and by 1899 was influential enough to convince Queen Victoria to ban the army from wearing Osprey plumes. In 1903, it began its regular magazine entitled *Bird Notes and News* (later just *Birds* and ultimately *Nature's Home*), and by 1930 had purchased its first nature reserve at Cheyne Court, Kent, bought for its rich Romney Marsh water meadows, which had unfortunately been drained of both water and conservation usefulness by 1950, resulting in its sale.

The society's founding in the aristocracy and upper middle classes enabled considerable influence over the makers of legislation in Parliament almost immediately, and key laws, prosecutions and fines over issues such as the import of wild bird feathers (1921), spillage of oil (1931) and the taking of wild birds for aviculture (1934) began highlighting the importance of conservation in both government and public consciousness.

Lessons were learned rapidly, and reserves continued to be founded with the opening of Dungeness, Kent, and Eastwood, Cheshire, in 1930. Perhaps the first real direct conservation success was the return of the Avocet as a British breeding bird simultaneously at Havergate and the flagship Minsmere reserve in 1947; the species was later adopted as the society's symbol in 1955. The famous and popular Osprey Hide at Loch Garten opened in 1959, at which point the RSPB had over 10,000 members; it took only a decade to achieve five times this figure. A decade later there were over 300,000 paid-up members, with 100,000 of these being under 16 and in the Young Ornithologists' Club (see pages 140-141).

1979 also saw the launch of the RSPB's first Big Garden Birdwatch, introducing the society into the vanguard of 'citizen science' which has proved so important in monitoring many changes in Britain's birdlife. Further innovations were forthcoming, not least the

An early RSPB membership card from 1897, in an era when the charity did exactly what its name and card implied; today it is more of an all-round conservation organisation, as the interconnectedness of nature has become obvious to science and public alike.

largest ever land purchase by a British non-governmental organisation when the society bought Abernethy Forest in 1988 for £1.8 million, and the following year half a million people demonstrated their concern for birds by paying for RSPB membership. Land use reversal was also initiated at Lakenheath Fen, where large swathes of Suffolk carrot fields and former poplar forestry were bought to convert back to their original habitat of extensive reedbeds and riverine woodland.

A protracted campaign begun in 1996 finally had the result of RSPB membership reaching the milestone figure of a million individuals in 1997, though the number has risen little since. The reasons for this are unclear, but it may be partly the case that it is only this proportion of the British public which has an active interest in birds and their conservation, with incoming younger members balancing out the deaths of older. That said, a

million members is a hefty wedge of positive environmental opinion to throw at legislators and others, and the RSPB's position as Britain's most popular and important conservation body remains unchallenged and much imitated abroad.

Its reach over the last 20 years has involved promoting and conserving 'our' bird species at their wintering and foreign breeding sites, as well as liaising with many other national and international organisations, notably via collaborations with BirdLife International, whom it represents in the UK. Today its influence is more wide-ranging and powerful than ever before, influencing governmental decisions over energy, land use, agriculture, and industrial and construction developments, as well as carving out a significant section of the spending muscle of the 'green pound', the purchasing power of which can frequently speak louder than mere protest.

36 : Mortensen bird ring

1890

Bird ringing, or banding as it is known in North America, has proved to be the best way to reveal the international wanderings of birds as they migrate, for more than a century providing much-needed information on behaviour and conservation needs as well as distribution.

Birds have been marked in various ways since Roman times, when documentation dated to around 218-201 BC shows that officers during the Punic Wars were already using trained crows to convey messages attached to threads. Medieval falconers attached small discs holding their seal to their birds, while Royal swans had their ownership denoted after about 1560 by a nick or 'swan mark' on the bill. The legendary John James Audubon (see pages 46–47) also proved in 1803 that his local Eastern Phoebes returned to their birthplace by attaching silver cords to their legs as chicks.

However, it fell to a Danish school teacher to pioneer ringing as a method of discovering more about the movements of birds. Hans Christian Cornelius Mortensen (1856-1941) trapped Starlings in nestboxes in 1890, using self-designed 'snappers' or pliers and fitting home-made and labelled aluminium rings onto the birds. He then graduated onto White Storks and ducks, species known to migrate and also accessible for trapping. The novelty of the idea led to many of his recoveries being reported by local newspapers.

Ornithologists were quick to cotton on, and in 1902 Paul Bartsch began the first organised banding scheme in North America, when he ringed more than 100 Black-crowned Night Herons for the Smithsonian Institution. Another American, Jack Miner, banded more than 20,000 Canada Geese between 1909 and 1939, quickly establishing the importance of collecting mass data when the rings were returned by hunters.

In Britain, two ringing schemes were 'hatched' in 1909, with one run by the fledgling journal *British Birds* (see pages 96-97), instigated by its editor Harry Forbes Witherby, and another at Aberdeen University, started by Arthur Landsborough Thomson. A third scheme, organised by *Country Life* magazine, also started at this time, but the rings were not uniquely numbered.

The Aberdeen scheme ended during the First World War, and in the 1930s, following the founding of the British Trust for Ornithology, the *British Birds* scheme was transferred to the BTO, which continues to administer the national ringing programme in Britain today.

Although recovery rates are very low, over time the sheer volume of birds ringed has led to truly revelatory discoveries. One of the first mysteries of migration to be solved was when a female Swallow, ringed as a chick in Staffordshire in May 1911 by John Masefield, a

Danish ornithologist Hans Mortensen (left) first fitted metal rings to birds, and ringing continues now in a very similar fashion (right), though on a far wider scale.

local solicitor, was recaptured (or 'controlled' in ringing parlance) in the Natal region of South Africa on 12 December the following year.

In 1919, von Lucanus reviewed more than 3,000 controls of 127 bird species, noting a pattern that indicated several distinct European 'flyways'. The first migration atlas was published in 1931 by Schütz and Weigold, and presented data from more than 6,800 controls of 230 species, covering the whole of Europe, North Africa and the Middle East – the Western Palearctic.

In practical terms, the development of ringing pliers in the mid-1970s by Bert Axell, then warden of Dungeness RSPB reserve in Kent, was a quiet revolution. But the main innovation in ringing was in the early 1950s, when mist nets were first used, enabling the relatively harmless capture or recovery of small to medium-sized landbirds. They could be combined with fixed-frame Heligoland traps (see pages 192–193), while more robust cannon nets were soon introduced for bigger species like larger waders and gulls.

The increasing number of European ringing schemes was co-ordinated under the umbrella of the European Union for Bird Ringing (EURING) in the mid-1960s. Bird ringers undergo lengthy supervised training programmes administered by their national schemes before they can undertake the highly skilled business of extricating fragile, fluttering migrants from the mesh of nets and then weighing, measuring and ringing them – the welfare of the birds is always paramount.

Today, birds are ringed chiefly with numbered metal rings, and for specific studies sometimes with coloured plastic ('darvic') rings – often in combination with metal rings – though wing tags and bill saddles are still used for larger species such as raptors and ducks, and birds from captive breeding and reintroduction projects. Much data is still being gleaned on the nature of bird navigation, migration strategy, survival rates and estimations of population size, and the information from recoveries is an invaluable research and conservation tool.

Although the practice may eventually be superseded as radio and satellite transmission and tracking technology becomes cheaper and more widely available, the controlling and recovery of ringed birds continues to add vital detail to our knowledge of bird dispersal.

37 : The Complete Works of William Shakespeare

1890

In *Sur la Naturalisation des Animaux Utiles* — aka *On the Naturalisation of Useful Animals* (1849) — groundbreaking French biologist Isidore Geoffroy Saint-Hilaire produced copious convincing economic and proto-ecological arguments for the French government to introduce potentially beneficial animals and plants from the newly discovered and exploited colonies, mostly to control agricultural pests and provide different kinds of meat. He then founded the Société Zoologique d'Acclimatation (1854) to promote these ideas.

Saint-Hilaire's robust evangelising soon influenced the formation of other similar societies across the western world, including in 1871 the American Acclimatization Society (AAS), which had the expressed goal of introducing "useful or interesting" animals and plants to North America, and proceeded to promote itself with some zeal. By 1877 it had attempted to introduce Skylark, Common Starling, Pheasant and Japanese Grosbeak into Central Park, New York City. This wasn't the first such attempt at introductions — House Sparrows had already become possibly the commonest bird in the city, after eight pairs were freed in Brooklyn in 1851 — but they were the most ideologically driven, persistent and pernicious release of alien species.

The AAS's chairman in 1877 was a local pharmacist named Eugene Schieffelin, an amateur Shakespeare scholar who is suspected to have been behind the possibly apocryphal idea that every species of bird mentioned in the complete works of the Bard should be introduced to the United States of America — an alleged 600 or more of them. Most of the society's introductions didn't take, but both House Sparrow and Common Starling mirrored the progress of colonising settlers, spreading from New York to western Canada, California and Florida by the 1950s. The sparrow population peaked at more than 150 million in the 1950s, but is now in decline, while the starling population — after Schiefflin initially released the species in 1890 (hence the year of inclusion of this older work here) — has topped 200 million this century.

The damage done by these two species is only partially known, as the naïveté that led to the introductions in the first place was also reflected in the lack of information about native North American species available for comparison with modern data. However, they are both known to be agricultural pests, and Common Starling has certainly competed with Yellow-bellied Sapsucker for nest holes. Still, the influence of most European species appears to have been absorbed by the native American avifauna, as it had already robustly evolved to

It is alleged that more than 600 species are mentioned in the works of Shakespeare, and Eugene Shieffelin had the ill-conceived idea of trying to introduce them all to North America in the late 19th century; fortunately he failed, but not before House Sparrow and Starling had increased to plague numbers in some areas.

suit a temperate continental biota and climate, like its European rivals.

Where introduced species really do damage is on islands, which have frequently evolved entire radiations of birds, isolated and free from competition. The mid-Pacific state of Hawai'i has lost dozens of unique bird species since being colonised by Polynesians over 1,000 years ago, and even more after Europeans settled. Modern visitors to the archipelago could be forgiven for thinking they had walked into the world's largest aviary: Java Sparrows from South-East Asia, Yellow-fronted Canaries from East Africa and Black Francolins from the Middle East can all be seen.

Those Hawaiian honeycreepers – a very varied finch radiation – that have not become extinct have mostly been forced into the uplands by loss of habitat and cagebird-derived avian pox. Even there, they share their rainforest with Japanese White-eyes and Mariana Swiftlets from the south-west Pacific.

Birders and ornithologists – usually keen to see or study 'pure' wild species – cope with these introductions by categorising them as escapes, exotics or self-sustaining populations. Even species in this last category are frequently reliant on continued reintroductions (probably the case with Pheasant in Britain) or the proximity of humans, or they exponentially expand their populations until they run out of food or habitat – the west Asian Varied Tit performed this boom-and-bust feat following its introduction on Hawai'i. In fact, it is entirely possible to enjoy such introductions as wild birds adapting and changing as nature always does, while being aware of their potentially destructive influence, and they are also valid study subjects to assess how evolution copes with an alien presence.

38 : Telephoto lens

1891

The rapid expansion of photography in the 20th century meant that specimen hunting and the field skills learnt for the stalking of game and trophies could gradually be adapted to the less harmful observation of birds and the shooting of images. The post-war acquisitive hobbies of listing and twitching could also be said to have partly replaced trophy hunting.

But even birders with the best field skills are still only able to get face-to-face with their quarry very rarely, and it was the evolution of magnifying lenses that enabled feather-by-feather details to be captured forever by photographers.

The principles of the telephoto lens were initially theorised in Johannes Kepler's *Dioptrice* (1611), but became more fully realised in 1834 when military mathematician Peter Barlow created a prototype. Perhaps the first true and practical model was developed by Thomas Dallmeyer in 1891, though a few other engineers made similar lenses almost simultaneously. Their use remained specialised until the 1960s, when the popularisation of single lens reflex (SLR) cameras brought them within the reach and ability of press and sports photographers, as well as bird photographers.

The lenses needed to photograph birds up close can be divided into three broad types: telephoto, in which the length of the actual lens is shorter than the focal length (the distance over which light rays converge into a focus point within the lens tube); zoom, in which the focal length is varied to allow close-up or more distant shots; and long-focus, which has but one internal lens element and needs a long body to allow the light rays to coalesce on the focal point (these remaining at a single length and therefore a single magnification). This last lens type has become less frequently used by hobbyist birders in favour of the flexibility that can be gained from telephoto and, especially, zoom lenses.

The overall effect of both is magnification of the image, like having a telescope attached to a camera, a set-up now literally possible with digiscoping (see pages 190–191). A telephoto lens is constructed from more than one lens, unlike a fixed focal length camera lens, allowing truncation of the focal length within a shorter lens body by changing the angle of the light rays' paths onto smaller lenses.

The focal length of a zoom lens can be varied either parfocally, by sustaining focus as the lens zooms in and out, or varifocally,

Early telephoto lenses such as these produced by H. Dallmeyer
were expensive and specialised until the popularisation of SLR
cameras in the 1960s enabled much more widespread usage.

meaning refocusing is needed as the focal length changes. Zooms were first developed in telescopes, being described in 1834, but the first use in a camera was documented in 1902 by the US Patents Office, registered to Clile Allen. First manufactured in 40-120 mm format in 1932 for cinema film cameras, zoom lenses only came into mass production for still cameras in 1959, and again were popularised during the 1960s for the more affordable SLRs.

The elusiveness and/or distance of birds in the field has meant that such lenses have become a real boon, and it is now common to see birders as well as photographers carrying them alongside a multitude of other gadgetry. The days when birders would throw 'bins' and book in a bag and go birding are long gone, it seems, as indeed are the days when a sketch and a description would confirm a difficult identification or record – now only a photo will do.

39 : Porro-prism binocular

1894

What birder would be seen — or indeed see anything — without his or her trusty 'bins'? The binocular is a birding essential, as crucial as a pair of ears and more necessary than even a field guide. And not only do those reliable double handfuls bring birds closer, their invention and evolution could also be said to have driven the development of birding as a hobby, in a mutual marriage of tool and usage.

Binoculars are essentially two identical telescopes aligned physically and through a single focusing system, and designed to be held in both hands. The slightly differing viewpoints of each eye give the impression of depth to the image, a convincing illusion of three dimensions.

Original binoculars — which literally were two small-magnification telescopes joined together — are termed Galilean and have a convex objective lens and a concave eyepiece lens. Such a construction formed the basic design of opera glasses and other earlier-19th century optics.

Perhaps the first binocular revolution was the invention of porro-prism binoculars, but like all revolutions, it didn't happen overnight. In 1854 Ignazio Porro, an Italian optician, patented his system of twice-reflecting an

image in internal mirrors so that it retained its natural orientation to the eye, but it wasn't commercially developed until 1894, when Carl Zeiss began selling the first recognisably modern binocular.

Porro-prism binoculars are generally small, and have a bright and true image. The design stayed popular through to the late 20th century, but their industry primacy — at least in birding terms — was gradually usurped by roof-prism models. Roof prisms first emerged in the 1870s and were successfully commercially patented in 1905, again by Carl Zeiss. The direct alignment of lenses in roof-prism binoculars means that the barrels could be slimmer and more compact, but lose a little comparative brightness (though this can be compensated for in other ways such as lens coatings in modern models).

The continued use of binoculars for sports and birding, particularly that of roof-prism models, has resulted in many technical innovations during their evolution. Anyone who has ever tried to focus on a dim and distant bird in cold temperatures, drizzle or outright rain will, for example, appreciate the development of waterproofing and fog-proofing. Commercial hermetic sealing of

Porro-prism binoculars were an improvement on opera glasses, and
utilised a small series of mirrors aligned inside the wide body. The same
basic design remains in use today, though in the eyes of many birders they
have been superseded by more compact roof-prism models.

binoculars, which prevents water from getting inside, and gas-filling, to enable fog-proofing, date from the early 1970s. A waterproof binocular will have O-rings at each opening in its structure which aid focusing and act as internal washers, and the entire space inside is filled with gas (often nitrogen) by injection, then completely sealed.

The nitrogen chemically prevents the condensation caused by extreme changes and juxtapositions of temperature. The absence of oxygen negates corrosion on the optics' internal workings. However, even now, it is impossible to prevent all the actions of water vapour in optics, and users of even the most expensive brands will find that the minute amount of heat and water from their eyes will sometimes fog up their lenses in cold weather. Rubber armour typically completes the sealing of a binocular, preventing internal water access

and damage, as well as protecting the outer casing. Most are also tested underwater to see if both the rubber armour and metal housing can withstand pressure of up to 5m for five minutes, avoiding damage and water intrusion.

The optics market is now crowded with budget, mid-price and high-end options, with several major brands competing for the high-spending birder. Innovation remains ongoing, providing ever clearer, truer and brighter images for the field birder, while top-end models are sometimes worn as status symbols to mark the supposed skills of individual birders themselves.

Such precision optics have certainly aided the eyesight and expertise of many a birder. The development of the whole industry means that even entry-level binoculars can often be of a quality that only the best and most expensive could provide just a few short decades ago.

40 : Egg collection

1895

In an age of awareness of the rapidly declining populations of many bird species, those who indulge in the collecting of wild birds' eggs are now viewed harshly, and held to account by law. However, in the 19th century the quasi-science of oology, along with shooting, was one of the few ways in which early bird enthusiasts could get closer to and understand their subjects.

While the beauty of birds' eggs inspired much acquisitiveness, there was originally a scientific purpose to many collections, enabling the accumulation of research collections in museums for use in studying the variation and structure of the external part of birds' reproductive mechanisms. The Natural History Museum retains some 610,000 eggs in its collection, though that figure is surpassed by more than 800,000 eggs at the Western Foundation of Vertebrate Zoology in California, this quintessentially British practice being exported to the United States in the late Victorian era.

Although egging is often regarded as the habit of a bygone age of naturalists, and condemned by the British Ornithologists' Union back in 1908, it shouldn't be forgotten that in more naïve times in the 20th century, even some of the older generation of today's active birders first expressed their interest by stealing the clutches of local common birds, and accruing at least a small collection.

Many tree-climbing, apple-scrumping, bruise-kneed small boys learnt that the eggs should be 'blown' to prevent the yolks from spoiling. This involved using a small thorn or drawing pin to make a tiny hole in the more pointed end of the egg and a slightly larger hole in the base of the egg; the pin or thorn was pushed into the membranes and yolk repeatedly to break it up, and then the lips or a straw would be gently placed against the smaller of the two holes and the contents gradually blown out. Latterly, an acid solution is often put into the eggs to dissolve the embryo, as egg theft cannot be timed precisely with the earliest part of the bird's laying cycle.

The ease with which a collection could be self-started meant that by the mid-20th century most collectors were literally amateurs, and willing to take quite severe risks to obtain a rare egg, though the value of the actual eggs was no longer particularly high. The Protection of Birds Act 1954 made it illegal to collect eggs of the majority of British species, and it became against the law to even possess wild bird eggs after the passing of the Wildlife and Countryside Act 1981. In Britain, offences against these laws carry a maximum fine of £5,000 and a possible sentence of six months. These changes in the law and a growing awareness of the conservation implications of the activity undoubtedly affected its popularity, but for many the advent of good-quality, affordable modern optics provided a more

An egg collection is perhaps the poor man's mineral and gem drawer, and it is easy to
see the attraction of the intricately patterned ovoids. However, such collections are
indefensible and illegal in the modern age, when many bird species are declining.

acceptable means of getting close to nature.

Those remaining practitioners could be said to operate in a perverse parallel to mainstream birders, and a few are even birdwatchers themselves. The attractions of 'egging' are apparent in that it provides excitement, subterfuge, expertise and competition, and covertness is always attractive to a certain segment of society. Eggers have their own club in the Jourdain Society, named after the British ornithologist Rev. Francis Jourdain, though the aims of at least some of their members who have convictions for egg theft or possession are somewhat more acquisitive than study alone. Bird eggs are certainly beautiful and varied objects, often hard to obtain and fragile and precious to hold.

Many of the egging old guard are unashamed and openly documented in *The Egg Collectors of Great Britain and Ireland: an Update* by A C Cole and W M Trobe (Peregrine Books, 2011), and many also have maintained membership of the Jourdain Society to this day. One notorious egg thief of the modern era, Colin Watson, died in 2006, shortly after falling from a larch after investigating a nest; he was once accused of attempting to cut down a tree containing an Osprey's eyrie with a chainsaw. The RSPB has a list of about 300 extant egg collectors and clubs, though not all can be proved to be currently active.

EDITOR'S NOTE: *the date for this object, and therefore its correct place in the book's running order, is somewhat arbitrary, but nevertheless appropriate. Most objects bear the year of date of first use or invention, but it is difficult to ascribe a precise date to the first 'oological' egg collection in the sense intended here. So 1895 has been chosen to represent a time when egg-collecting was popular on both sides of the Atlantic.*

41 : Answering machine

1898

Before today's advanced array of communications gadgets and services, finding out 'what's about' or announcing the arrival or presence of rare birds meant reliance on a commonplace but ingenious household device: the telephone answering machine.

While it would be some time before such equipment was commandeered for keen birders, the first known answering machine was created in 1898 by Danish engineer Valdemar Poulsen. His 'telegraphone' used a wire to record on which passed a recording head to receive a magnetic signal that replicated a sound wave. The wire was later replaced by tape or disks, which served the very same function almost until the present day.

Telegraphones and their successors had to be manually operated, and it was not until the early 1930s that automatic answering machines were developed. The first commercially available machine was the American 'Tel-Magnet' which appeared in the shops in 1949, but the expense of this machine was successfully undercut by the introduction of Phonetel's 'Ansafone'.

This affordable, practical and popular device spawned many imitations and improvements, and really began to take off in 1960 for business and the more well-off private customer. However, it was still to be some years before such devices became truly household items. The presence of an answering machine on the credits of the TV detective series *The Rockford Files*, for example, was still enough to excite much workplace and school playground comment in 1974.

Initially a reel-to-reel tape loop provided the machine's answering message from its owner, but the development of the 'microcassette' enabled messages to play from beginning to end and then record the caller's own voice in response.

Unsurprisingly, the technology was adopted by birders as a semi-automated means of relaying news of rare and interesting species to local audiences. The heyday of the nascent bird news services was in the 1980s, though local news could be found on key numbers in some places in the 1970s; they were even still used occasionally in North America as news hubs at the turn of the century, notably in out-of-the-way sites in Alaska. All were usually at the

Despite being around for several decades beforehand, like this early unit
from 1898 (top), answering machines came into their own in the 1960s,
with cheap domestic and business machines becoming commonplace.

phone numbers of the local recorder or other luminary, and could often be at least a little out of date if not maintained.

Until the 1960s, rare bird sightings in Britain were largely reported by post, and the likelihood of a bird still being present once a postcard or letter had been received was slim. As the hobby of twitching developed through that decade, key people became the 'go-to guys'

for news, and several obtained answering machines for this purpose.

However, the sightings hub of Nancy's Café at Cley, Norfolk, had no answering machine in its hey-day in the 1970s and 1980s, relying on birders to answer the phone. This was to develop into one of the first bird news services, for which answerphone technology was key (see pages 146–147).

42 : Box Brownie budget camera

1900

The popularisation of bird photography has taken a long time, but cameras have been affordable and accessible for more than a century, with the Eastman Kodak Box Brownie in 1900 the first to open up photography to the masses and introduce the concept of the snapshot.

Brownies were originally little more than a glorified camera obscura (see pages 44-45), composed of a cardboard box, a simple lens and a roll of film. The Brownie brand was popular enough for the name to be retained even after the Second World War, by which time they were constructed from Bakelite and used Kodak's improved 120 and 127 films.

Such accessibility did not open up a world of amateur wildlife photography, prompting one blogger recently to recall: 'In 5th grade, I got a

simple Brownie box camera – just aim and click, and shoot. Unfortunately, the resulting bird photographs had a tiny black speck, which was the bird. My bird pictures became sort of a family joke: find the bird.'

Leica was the true innovator of portable cheap cameras, when the company thought of using 35mm cine film for the compact cameras it was prototyping as long ago as 1913. Kodak jumped on the bandwagon with its Retina I in 1934, and the Japanese quickly followed suit in 1936, when Canon entered the market.

However, it was the development of commercial single lens reflex cameras, coupled with the advent of telephoto lenses, that eventually opened up a world of more affordable bird photography for the less privileged (see pages 116–117).

AN EFFICIENT
5/-
FILM CAMERA.

THE BROWNIE.

Not a Toy. Takes splendid Photographs,
~~21 by 21~~ inches. Complete with Hand-
~~...tions.~~ Price only **5/-**

~~...alers,~~ *or from--*
~~...~~mited,
~~...~~oad, E.C.;
~~...~~E.C.;
~~...~~et, W.;
~~...~~ Street, W.

"Not a toy" – the first affordable commercial camera revolutionised
the average person's leisure hours and family time, as well as
empowering the first amateur bird photographers.

43 : *British Birds*

1907

As birding began to emerge as a recreational hobby in the late 19th century, a demand for accessible ornithological studies of the British avifauna developed. Networks of local birdwatchers became established and their common interests needed a forum for the discussion and recording of research and observations. These interests coalesced in 1907 with the first issue of *British Birds*.

A monthly periodical for 'serious' birdwatchers and ornithologists, it was founded by Harry Witherby and immediately filled a gap in the marketplace for an authoritative publishing hub of new research, and reviews of records and current knowledge. Though containing much conservation and ecological research, an underlying thrust was – and indeed remains – rarities, a fact underlined by a paper by Howard Saunders in the first issue entitled 'Additions to the List of British birds since 1899'. Note especially the capital 'L' on the word 'List' – 'BB', as it became widely known, stamped its authority on amateur ornithology in Britain and what was to be 'officially' counted from day one. It also popularised the use of the trinomial – the three-part scientific name – for subspecies, the limits of which still obsess birders to this day.

BB absorbed *The Zoologist* in 1916 to become the leading periodical of its kind for many decades. As the hobby increased in popularity, so did the public's interest in rare birds, and in 1959 the magazine established the British Birds Rarities Committee, a body comprising 10 expert adjudicators – originally dubbed 'the 10 rare men' – of rarity sightings that exists to this day and is still respected and followed by many birders. The committee has so far had 69 members since its inception.

Part magazine and part journal, *British Birds* dominated its field before the popularisation of birding in the 1980s, and in later years was published by Macmillan before entering private ownership and, latterly, becoming the product of its own charitable trust. Marking its milestone 100th year, in 2007 it released *BBi*, an interactive archive on DVD containing every article, photo and illustration it had ever published. Since then much historical material has also appeared on its website, cementing its contribution to birding and amateur ornithology in Britain online as well as in print.

BB's importance for those interested in

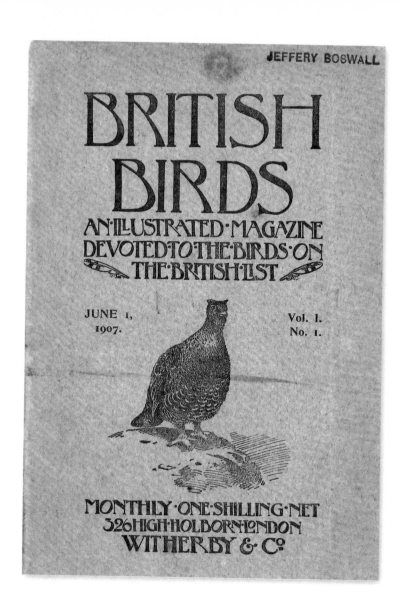

British Birds has retained its usefulness for both the regular
birder and the more scientifically inclined, as well as respect
for its authority in identification matters.

readable but scientifically informed in-depth
musings on identification, taxonomy and
associated subjects remains strong. Shrugging
off criticism of occasional alleged slowness in
accepting or rejecting rare bird records, its
eponymous rarities committee also maintains
the publication's authority in the British
birding scene.

44 : Map of breeding migrants

1909

A key early paper in *British Birds* was 'On a plan of mapping migratory birds in their nesting areas' (Alexander and Alexander, 1909). This contribution from came from two of three famous ornithological brothers: H G Alexander, who later authored *Seventy Years of Birdwatching* and lived to see his 100th birthday in 1989; and his brother Christopher, who died in Flanders in 1917. It contained ideas and methods that would become the root of birders' habitual counting and surveying of birds, and grow into the kind of citizen science that enables the success of many RSPB and BTO surveys to this day. It was the origin of systematic bird monitoring as we now know it.

A summary of two years' worth of extensive private survey work carried out around Tunbridge Wells, Kent, their data and map demonstrated the local changes in population of summering bird species. They showed that visiting breeders were territorial, and were able to estimate each species' breeding population accordingly; in effect, they had invented a kind of common bird census years before the British Trust for Ornithology (BTO).

After organising an Oxford bird census in 1927, a year later Max Nicholson used *British Birds* to organise and initiate the first count of British heronries – the most comprehensive survey of a single species at the time. He published the prescient results and conclusions in that same periodical in 1929.

It was obvious now that the growing legions of amateur birdwatchers could be corralled into accumulating useful scientific and conservation data. *British Birds* had occasionally ruminated on founding a national ornithological research organisation for the disparate and localised data being gathered around the country, and by 1933 this idea had finished its gestation. Nicholson, Bernard Tucker and Wilfred Alexander – the third brother – formed the BTO in partnership with Oxford University.

The trust has operated ever since as an independent generator of and clearing house for ornithological research (it being 'uncongenial' for Britain to have a governmental body performing such a service, Nicholson wrote in 1931). Particular emphasis is still placed on population surveys, and ringing has played a motivational importance, the BTO not only granting ringers' licences through its ad hoc training programme but co-ordinating single species surveys and the Constant Effort Site scheme.

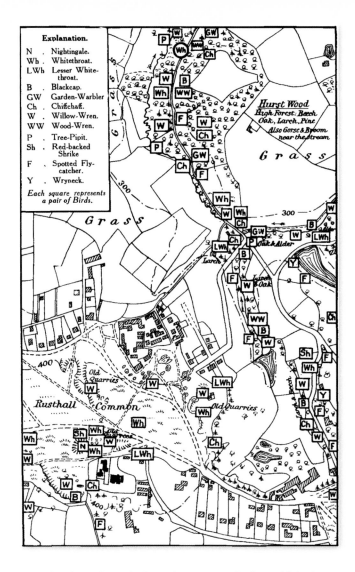

The Alexander and Alexander map was the first published
illustration of the comprehensive results of a local bird survey
– simple in its execution but highly influential to this day.

For many years the BTO was based at Tring, Hertfordshire, but a 1991 move to donated premises and land in Thetford, Norfolk, enabled it to establish a new headquarters and even maintain its own nature reserve. The organisation has achieved a more public profile in recent years, capitalising on the mass appeal of projects such as 'observer inclusive' atlas fieldwork and a fascinating Common Cuckoo radio-tracking programme which has generated extraordinary new findings about the species. Arguably, however, the origins of much of its work which is derived from data gathered in the field can be traced back more than a century to a map drawn by two brothers in the borough of Tunbridge Wells.

45 : Aeroplane ticket

1911

Before the availability of commercial air flights, foreign birding was still largely the preserve of the well-off and the sponsored, and to experience the birds of other continents those of modest incomes and connections were best served by joining the armed forces or the merchant navy.

The first commercial flight took place in 1911, but it wasn't until 1926 that this mode of transport was finally viewed as affordable and safe. In the USA, subsidies to encourage mail flights to take passengers and fairly strict safety regulations to build customer confidence meant that, by 1930, there was a flourishing and recognisable air industry. United Airlines featured stewardess service by trained nurses who also balanced mechanical repairs, refuelling and cleaning of the aircraft with their in-flight duties, including the serving of meals and drinks.

With a booming airline industry in the post-war years, the door was open for overseas holidays specifically to watch birds. In 1965, Lawrence Holloway set up such a trip under the banner of Ornitholidays to Camargue, France – a bird-rich area very much viewed as an exotic location in pre-package tour days. This was quickly followed by an Austrian trip,

thereby establishing a still burgeoning market for specialist birding holidays and what are now often known as ecotours.

Some companies emphasise the holiday aspect almost as much as the birds and wildlife, but with the growing popularity of world listing, and obsessed birders realising it is now actually possible to see most of the world's bird species, other companies have established more 'hardcore' reputations with itineraries which concentrate on getting as many 'ticks' as possible.

In essence, though, the broad concept of ecotourism began perhaps a decade before that first Ornitholidays venture, and can be traced to the formalisation of game hunting in the 1950s when the market for recreational shooting of trophy wildlife led to the demarcation of game reserves, protected wildlife areas and national parks in some of the countries of sub-Saharan Africa. The idea of ecotourism is now long divorced from its uneasy arranged marriage with the big game hunter, though such 'sport' remains popular in certain quarters, and many reserves are still maintained with this purpose in mind, incidentally protecting local wildlife.

In some areas, however, reserve operators

Commercial flying is now becoming more expensive, but for a few
decades it has been cheap enough to open up the globe to almost
anyone willing to explore it, including many thousands of birders.

now deem conservation more important than
hunting, with the latter viewed as a necessary
evil. In 2013 Zambia finally banned big cat
hunting, its tourist minister Sylvia Masebo
stating: "Tourists come to Zambia to see the
Lion and if we lose the Lion we will be killing
our tourism industry. Why should we lose our
animals for $3 million a year? The benefits we
get from tourist visits are much higher."

Birding contributes billions of dollars to
different countries' economies – its popularity
in the USA alone is estimated to generate $24
billion and employ more than 60,000 people.
In many parts of bird-rich Africa and South

America, bird guides who have turned their
innate local ornithological knowledge –
sometimes derived from hunting skills – into
real expertise are among the high earners in
their local communities, injecting cash into
their area and providing secondary
employment in tourist services.

Birders are at the forefront of the
dissemination of ecological awareness on a
global scale, and can also be said to be
spreading a kind of grass roots diplomacy, an
international understanding at a personal
level, travelling further into countries and
regions than even many backpackers.

46 : Public telephone box

1920

Ever since Alexander Graham Bell patented its invention in 1876, the telephone has been of paramount importance in communications. Its use in birding escalated away from casual communication when twitching really began to catch on, most notably from the late 1970s and 1980s onwards, and the urgent reporting of rare bird sightings became necessary for this sub-hobby to be pursued effectively. In the days before mobile phones, regular stops at public phone boxes became an essential activity on twitches, either to find out if a bird was still present, or to report a sighting to others.

To a significant extent at that time, the unofficial grapevine on which competitive birding depended centred on the twin Norfolk hubs of Nancy's Café, Cley (see pages 146–147), and nearby Walsey Hills NOA reserve. Both were key birding assembly points which had unofficial hotlines that birders would regularly ring for news. By the mid-1980s this cottage communications industry took firm root with the establishment of Birdline, a name originally coined by Walsey Hills warden

Roy Robinson, and the Bird Information Service's Bird Alert. Initially using periodically updated answering machine messages listing rare bird sightings and access details, the services became popular and soon merged.

The resulting operation, which retained the Birdline name, went on to adopt a premium rate telephone number and then spawn a network of regional bird news franchises. Refining the concept still further, in 1991 Norwich-based Rare Bird Alert introduced a national paging service (see pages 178–179), while for many others the internet took over around the turn of the century as the BirdGuides.com website and its different web-based alerts soared in popularity.

But for all the competition in the bird news market, it's clear that there remains a role for phones, as mobile handsets (see pages 148–149) become more and more sophisticated and services like Twitter increase the potential for using them in various ways in the 'sport' of birding.

Finding a red telephone box in pre-mobile days was a
constant bind when trying to put out the news of a rarity
or, later, phoning a bird news service; many have now
been sold off, scrapped or fallen into disrepair.

47 : Milk bottle top

1921

Birds are not just the ever-elusive objects of their observers' desires to collect ticks on a list, or representations of their beholders' need to have specialist or secret knowledge — many draw immediate attention to themselves or exploit humans' own environments and products.

This is nature's way, of course, but it is also perhaps why most people, whether habitual birdwatchers or just appreciators of nature in the broadest sense, feel some kind of connection to the presence and activities of birds. They share human space in ways which are described in biology as parasitic (where one party profits to the detriment of the other), symbiotic (a mutually beneficial relationship) or commensal (where one party benefits without detriment to the other).

Birds inhabit and exploit farms, gardens and homes all around the world. There are many campaigns to combat the decline of farmland birds brought about by intensive agriculture, though their remembered numbers are very much artificial in themselves, products of the adaptation of scrub and woodland-edge species to the patchwork of habitats created by the development of arable land in the first place. The even bigger picture

is that farmland is also mitigation for the wholesale destruction of woodlands and their 'edge' habitats, as Britain and Europe was rapidly deforested over the last 2,000 years or so.

A now-rare and prosaic example of birds' lives interweaving with humans is the phenomenon of cream stealing. The 'milk snatchers' in this case were not acolytes of Margaret Thatcher but some of our most common garden birds: Blue and Great Tits, and Robin. Birds cannot digest lactose-rich cows' milk but, given the opportunity, will enjoy the lactose-free cream. This habit was perhaps originally developed in the late 19th century when they raided domestic dairy deliveries, but first properly documented in 1921 when birds described as tits were seen to prise open the wax-board tops of bottles on doorsteps in Swaythling, near Southampton.

The pre-war provision of aluminium caps on milk bottles — with colour codes of gold (cream-rich Guernsey and Jersey milk), silver (whole milk), red (homogenised), red and silver (semi-skimmed) and so forth — provided only temporary respite from the depredations of otherwise insectivorous birds; with their sharp beaks they were easily able to peck

The rapidity with which Blue and Great Tits discovered how to peck through the aluminium foil caps of traditional glass milk bottles to access the cream demonstrated how quickly knowledge of a food source can spread among wild birds; the introduction of waxed cardboard cartons showed how quickly it can be lost.

through to the cream below, the bottle lip acting as a handy perch. Robins developed the skill locally, but the habit spread through the national populations of both tit species.

With changes in milk consumption preferences, the decline of doorstep milk deliveries and the widely adopted switch in milk packaging to plastic bottles and Tetrapaks, the phenomenon has virtually died out. Today's garden birds rely far more on bird feeders than the almost non-existent prospect of free doorstep cream. However, the rise and fall of the cream thieves emphasises the malleability of our most familiar avian neighbours as they perform the dance of adaptation around our own changing habits.

48 : Swiftlet's nest

1922

Among the multitude of interesting ingredients in Oriental cookery are the nests of a few species of cave swiftlet, opaque cups of congealed saliva that are among the most expensive animal-derived delicacies. This 'caviar of the east' has been used in Chinese cookery for at least 400 years, and when dissolved in water makes a glutinous soup alleged to improve digestion, improve the immune system and – inevitably – act as an aphrodisiac.

The nests, most commonly of the Edible-nest Swiftlet, contain the same ovotransferrin protein as egg white, and are traditionally collected from the walls of limestone caves in Borneo. However, the lucrative trade has meant that many are now harvested from specially built reinforced concrete nesting houses in more widespread locations in South-East Asia, and the swiftlets' colonial presence has led to boom towns growing where subsistence villages once stood.

Who could begrudge local people lifting themselves out of poverty by exploiting a remunerative natural resource to be found in their native towns? It was an easily harvested and readily prepared commodity that commanded high enough prices to be viewed as a bourgeois indulgence during the Chairman Mao era, and now a new generation of Chinese *nouveau riche* are keen to import it at a premium.

Perhaps conservationists could begrudge that kind of tradition. Far from being a sustainable local practice, it had a significant impact in some places. Colonies in the Andaman Islands, for example, have been significantly over-exploited, causing the locally endemic subspecies of Edible-nest Swiftlet to be listed by the International Union for the Conservation of Nature as Critically Endangered.

The temptation to over-collect or harvest too early for impoverished islanders with little other source of income often proves too much hindrance for the introduction of sustainable harvesting methods. The Indian government which administers the Andamans has made Edible-nest Swiftlet one of its most highly protected birds, but the difficulties of guarding remote nest sites and the fact that collectors are well rewarded enough to even risk death means that the population of the birds has barely recovered over the last decade.

Overall, there is a substantial export trade of swiftlet nests mostly through the hub of Hong Kong to countries such as Japan, South

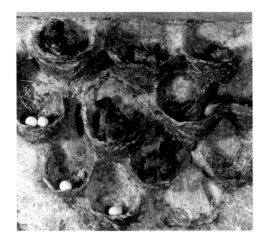

The over-exploitation of Edible-nest Swiftlet colonies shows
how quickly the demands of human free trade can deplete
unique wild populations of bird species.

Korea, Taiwan, Singapore, Canada and the
USA, much of which is legal as the major
species are listed as Least Concern on the
worldwide criteria used by the IUCN and
BirdLife International.

But aspects of the Edible-nest Swiftlet case
encapsulate many of the problems of modern
conservation, with their geographical,
cultural, taxonomic and economic reach.
Though the species is widespread and common
in places, exploitation of its nests has caused
has caused a decrease in numbers, rather
marked in some genetically unique
populations, and international legislation is
incomplete, has been partly ignored or cannot
be enforced where it is most needed.

Historically, the exploitation of bird species,
from encouraging House Sparrows to breed for
easily accessible eggs and chicks on the one
hand to the profligate hunting of dozens of
colourful or exotic species merely for their
plumes on the other, has actually inspired

modern bird conservation as we know it. And
this tricky balance, constantly buffeted by
human changes, will continue as ecosystems
and biodiversity are now discussed in pseudo-
or actual economic terms and contexts.

The human exploitation of birds on an
international scale, symbolised here by the tiny
nest of *Collocalia fuciphaga*, needed a cross-border
organisation to try to prevent the loss of global
avian biodiversity and reach beyond the limits
of country-specific organisations. It was to
lobby internationally in this way that American
ornithologists T Gilbert Pearson and J T
Delacour formed the International Council
for Bird Preservation in 1922, this
organisation transforming into BirdLife
International in 1993. It exists to foster
co-operation between bird preservation
organisations throughout the world, bolstering
their efforts, pooling resources and expertise,
and – most importantly of all – speaking out
globally on behalf of birds with a single voice.

49 : Road sign

1923

The notion of travelling to see birds, rare or otherwise, would be mere smoke without a well-connected and well-maintained road network. Cars, very much a luxury at the beginning of the last century, are now integral to so many aspects of modern life, and birding is no exception.

The first private motor vehicle was registered on 3 July 1895, with several others following that year, but roads had hitherto been designed for horse traffic, either being topped with dry, dusty tar or very often being little more than dirt tracks, damped down by water trucks. Until the First World War, these were soon worn into disrepair in many places by heavy cars and steam-driven lorries.

The fact that the internal combustion engine would be the mode of transport of the 20th century was, however, realised early on, and several prescient engineers advocated a safe and graded network of well-constructed roads for Britain, partly inspired by Italy's construction in 1921 of its first section of *autostrade*, which soon connected Milan and Varese. In Britain the Trunk Roads Act of 1936 enabled the government to control the country's connective arteries, and during the

1939–1945 war plans were drawn up for Britain's post-conflict economic recovery, with a new road system cited as a touchstone for this.

The expansion of Britain's roads was therefore only encouraged by the end of the Second World War, and the first listing of road numbers in 1923 was followed by the publication of the first projected map of what would become the motorway system in 1946 – this including the circular route of the putative M25. By 1958, the first 8.3 miles of the M6 was opened – the Preston by-pass – with the entire M1 opening the following year, providing a high-speed link from London to Birmingham. December 1965 saw the introduction of the 70 mph speed limit on the motorways.

Before such extensive road construction happened, the idea of travelling the length and breadth of the country to watch birds would have been inconceivable. Yet today cars and the freedom of movement they provide are for many an integral part of birding – along with the direct innovations in optics, books and telecommunications, the development of the road system has to be seen as a key background driver for the range and scope of the modern hobby as we know it.

The growth of birding as a popular pastime – and twitching as a competitive if disorganised sport – was greatly helped by the post-war development of the British and international road systems.

50 : Television set

1925

While the birds themselves must get the main credit for inspiring nascent birders and ornithologists, one of the greatest influences on interest in the natural world is the television wildlife documentary. Early films in the genre were screened at cinemas, but with the advent of television and the ability to broadcast them into the nation's living rooms, their influence spread rapidly and widely to a mesmerised new audience.

As with so many technological advancements that have enriched the hobby of birding, television has its roots in the late 19th century. One of the earliest key developments was Paul Nipkow's mechanical images 'scanning disk', composed of metal or card with holes placed evenly around it, showing slices of a scene or image and capable of capturing and converting motion to electric signals. Famously, John Logie Baird demonstrated moving images on his television in 1925 at Selfridge's in London, and within two years non-publicly available transatlantic images were being transmitted. A form of video – called 'phonovision' – had already been developed by Baird in 1927.

Limited programming was in place by 1930, and the BBC launched its first television service in 1932. Britain was the quickest to take

to the medium, despite the six-year interruption of the Second World War, and by 1947 there were 54,000 TV sets in the UK, 10,000 more than in the USA.

The natural history documentary had been evolving in parallel, and drew sizeable audiences at cinemas. Eadweard Muybridge's *Horse in Motion* (1882) was one of the most important early stepping stones to cinematography, while Percy Smith later astounded cinema audiences with his time-lapse *Birth of a Flower* in 1910.

The BBC entered the 1950s as an organisation already producing wildlife films, with *Coelacanth* by Julian Huxley (1952) its most notable early production, also earning David Attenborough his first credit. The following year saw Attenborough's first series, *The Pattern of Animals*, and in 1954 came the inaugural episode of *Zoo Quest*, which was to run for 10 years. This latter series was truly groundbreaking, taking the BBC and Attenborough all over the globe to such locations as New Guinea and West Africa, and providing real temptation for the ambitious birder, with programmes on hitherto little-seen birds-of-paradise and the still enigmatic White-necked Rockfowl. The bright variety

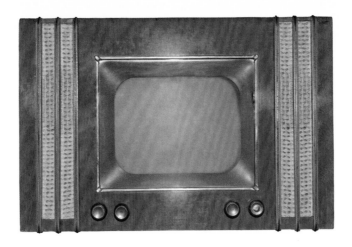

The first viewers of programmes like David Attenborough's *Zoo Quest* had to make do with tiny black and white screens, but this was enough to inspire a generation to begin travelling to more and more destinations to see their unique avifauna.

and exotica of the ornithological world was suddenly available to view in the entire country's front rooms.

Another early attempt to make all the earth a stage in a TV series was *Look*, Peter Scott's live wildlife broadcast for the BBC, often with the accent on birds and – unsurprisingly – wildfowl in particular. The BBC's Natural History Unit had been founded in 1957, and the most senior and iconic figure for the entirety of its existence has been Sir David Attenborough. The corporation's switch to colour in 1967 was overseen by Attenborough, in his then capacity as the controller of BBC2.

Sir David's series continue to unfold well into the 21st century, with many notable milestones including *Life on Earth* (1979) – showing the immensity of the world's interconnected ecosystems, as well as demonstrating the truth of evolution to many millions of 'agnostics' – and *The Life of Birds* (1998), which surely inspired many viewers to take an interest in the world's birds.

Another significant television birding evangelist in recent years is Bill Oddie. Though other presenters such as the late John Gooders raised birding's respectability in the 1960s and 1970s, it was the one-time member of TV comedy trio The Goodies who did the most to raise the hobby's profile above perceived geekdom, notably with *Birding with Bill Oddie* (1997-2000); the series visited many key birdwatching locations in Britain and around the world, giving millions a taste of the intrigue and excitement (and in some cases the privation) that birding can entail.

The extensive reach of the BBC's programming has changed attitudes towards wildlife to a more observational and conservation-led concern, and piqued interest worldwide, through licensing and global broadcasting. Birding is an outdoor hobby, despite its modern reliance on computers and mobile phones, but the influence of a well-filmed, bird-rich TV documentary on budding birders cannot be underestimated.

51 : Ernest Holt newspaper cutting

1928

The date of 7 April 1928 is not often mentioned in history books, but it has a hitherto unsung importance in ornithology's timeline. On this day, the National Geographic Society and Carnegie Institution announced that "foremost American authority on bird life" Ernest G Holt would lead an expedition to Venezuela to attempt to track down wintering populations of North America's summer visitors.

This was far from the first ever bird-seeking expedition, but it had a succinct difference: "In the course of his study," continued Florida's *St Petersburg Times*, "Holt will amass photographs and collections of such wonder birds as the scarlet ibis with its brilliant red plumage, which is the envy of the textile dye maker; the cock-of-the-rock, with its curious double crest ... and the ungainly jabiru stork ... which stands higher than our sandhill crane." Holt was embarking on the first ever bird photography trip.

Amass photographs he did, returning with specimens and images of more than 3,000 individuals of 486 species from his often perilous journey, greatly adding to what was then known about the variety and distribution of South American birds. There were already a number of bird and nature photography books dealing with western avifauna, including William Nesbitt's *How to Hunt with the Camera* (1926), and the hobby was growing domestically, but Holt was the first photographer to travel to an inaccessible destination specifically to at least partly document its birds. That he did this amid considerable logistical difficulty with a plate camera makes it a monumental achievement, and is even more to his credit.

Holt's life was remarkable in other ways. Not only was he an innovative and intrepid ornithologist and photographer, but his first major expedition was with Percy Fawcett in 1920, a character on whom the fictional cinematic archaeologist Indiana Jones was based. Holt fell out with Fawcett during the abortive and traumatising trek to the Amazon, and was not invited on Fawcett's next expedition, during which he disappeared for good, creating a press sensation at the time. Holt went on to have a brilliant career, both in the scientific world, publishing in *The Auk*, and in the public eye, writing about his travels for *National Geographic*.

AMERICAN EXPEDITION PLANS
TO STUDY VENEZUELAN BIRDS

TON, April 7.—The
ographic Society and
titution announced to-
expedition will be sent
s of Venezuela to dis-
ecomes of American
ke their winter homes
ore.

on will be headed by
lt, foremost American
rd life.
he original American
s their winter homes
nezuela which Holt's
ore.
ll leave the United
w Orleans where he
Guaira. When he
a largely unexplored
the broad Orinoco he
ces to penetrate the
country where one
lives and travelers
d back by hardships
.

is the major objec-
rations of the land,
ther life forms, and
ty of tropical trees
," Holt said.
-blithely overhead
avy of land-bound
complete freedom
birds have distinct-
nparable to wheat
lines, and it is by
tions of these life
pe to make an ex-
of the bird life of

a knows some
tanagare, for ex-
s originated in the
re familiar to tem-
Certain of the

West Indies islands which are rem-
nants of a former continental mountain chain are believed to have been
the highways for the dispersal of
various kinds of birds. Further
studies will determine these and
hundreds of other facts dear to the
student of bird lore, which facts also
may shed light upon the making
and changing over of our continent
at various geologic times."
In the course of his study Holt
will amass photographs and collections of such wonder birds as the
scarlet ibis with its brilliant red
plumage, which is the envy of the
textile dye maker; the cock-of-the-
rock, with its curious double crest
formed of two groups of feathers
pressed together, and the ungainly
jabiru stork, with its white plumage
and naked black head and neck,
which stands higher than our sandhill crane.
Venezuela is a happy hunting
ground of the ornithologist because
of its variety of climatic and physical zones, ranging from mountain
peaks that pierce the clouds at some
17,000 feet to the low plains along
the sluggish Orinoco.
However, the unexplored area,
lying between the Rio Caura and
Rio Branco, is a region of dense
forests.
There are many perils. This area
lies just north of the Brazilian bor-
der and east of the region where,
near the town of Esmeralda, the
giant basins of the Orinoco and the
Amazon so overlap that the flip of
a bird's wing may determine whether
a drop of rain will reach the sea
at the Orinoco's delta or flounder
halfway across the continent to
emerge at the island-flecked mouth
of the Amazon.

U. S. NATIONAL MUSEUM   PROCEEDINGS, VOL. 97   PLATE 27

Black-collared swallows (*Atticora melanoleuca*) on rock near Isla Yagrumo, Venezuela

Sun-bittern (*Eurypyga helios*) at San Antonio, Venezuela.

Further inspiration for the travelling birder and photographer
came from illustrated reports of bird-seeking expeditions like
those of Ernest Holt, which demonstrated the feasibility of seeing
and capturing for posterity near-mythical species like Sunbittern.

52 : Peterson field guide

1934

While there was no particular shortage of reference books in the early 20th century, these were generally unwieldy multi-volume works which perhaps reached their apogee with H F Witherby's *Practical Handbook of British Birds* (1938-41). For quick identification of a sighting in the field, enthusiasts had to rely on their memories, notebooks or, in those less enlightened times, their shotgun to 'collect' an unknown wild bird.

This was to change in 1934, when a young ornithologist named Roger Tory Peterson published *A Field Guide to the Birds*, the first pocket-sized and fairly comprehensive identification guide to the North American avifauna. This launched a whole series of field guides to the animals, plants and geology of the Nearctic, and the concept spread across the Atlantic in 1954 with *A Field Guide to the Birds of Britain and Europe,* co-authored with Guy Mountfort and P A D Hollom. The book featured Peterson's patented style of depicting both sexes, often in colour, with lines pointing out key field characteristics. Though there were objections to some of the plates being reproduced in black and white, the original book sold out its first run of 2,000 within a week, and has remained in print ever since.

There was clearly a need for such handy and comprehensive guides in the field. In Britain, the market soon had several widely variable choices aimed at the field observer. To this day,

many an older birder will confess a sentimental attachment to the incomplete and impractical *Observer's Book of British Birds* (S Vere Benson, 1945) or *Collins Pocket Guide to British Birds* (R S R Fitter and R A Richardson, 1954).

Such books were progress but also far from perfect, and many found the constant flipping back and forth between text and plates in Peterson in particular a little impractical. A further improvement in the format came with the publication of guides which featured the text for each species directly facing its illustration, including Bruun and Singer's *Birds of Europe* (1971) and Heinzel, Fitter and Parslow's more expansive *Birds of Britain and Europe with North Africa and the Middle East* (1972). Part of the achievement of the latter title was to encourage many budding birders to consider their native region biogeographically rather than geopolitically. Not only this but – especially in later revised editions – numerous hitherto obscure regional subspecies were also copiously listed and illustrated.

The increasing popularity of foreign bird trips also created a demand for guides to the birds of regions further afield, and Collins in particular led the market with its African and Australian guides (in addition to the rapid expansion into other forms of wildlife). The baton began to be passed to the Christopher Helm imprint with the 1983 publication of Peter Harrison's *Seabirds*, followed by the then

Roger Tory Peterson was a gifted bird artist and an innovative author who saw the now-obvious need for a portable, pocket-sized comprehensive guide to identifying the daunting number of bird species that can be observed in almost any region.

landmark *Birds of Europe* by Lars Jonsson in 1992, and the company has since come to dominate the global bird field guide market with its ever-expanding Helm Field Guides series.

By the late Nineties, European birders with increasing experience and skills were longing for even more. The extended gestation of the *Collins Bird Guide* (Svensson, Mullarney and Zetterström, 1999), covering much of the Western Palearctic, proved well worth the wait, with up-to-date taxonomy, structured layout of the plates and strikingly life-like figures of birds in most of their plumages. That was quickly followed by a new Nearctic benchmark, David Sibley's *The North American Bird Guide* (2000) – or *The Sibley Guide to Birds*, as it was titled in its native continent. It differed from the *Collins Bird Guide* in having little text, relying much more heavily on the author's jizzy but accurately

impressionistic illustrations to identify North American species.

Further field guide innovations include Nils van Duivendijk's *Advanced Bird ID Guide* (2010) with no illustrations but detailed bullet-point analysis of feathers and features of Western Palearctic species, Richard Crossley's *The Crossley ID Guide* (2011) with novel photo-montages of multiple individuals of each species set in typical habitat, and Bob Flood and Ashley Fisher's *Multimedia Identification Guide to North Atlantic Seabirds* series (from 2012), with its accompanying DVD-ROM of film footage along with forensic identification features.

Whether visiting a country or region, studying a family or group, or focusing on a particular habitat, birders are likely to be able to find precisely the right guide for their needs, a choice owed to Roger Tory Peterson.

53 : Leica SLR camera

1935

A giant step forward for photographers was the invention of the single lens reflex (SLR) camera, which enabled them to see through a viewfinder the image they were shooting exactly as it would appear on film.

Previously, cameras had to make do with the viewfinder and film not sharing the same optical path – that is, the path of light through the lens – but the positioning of a mirror and prism between the lens and the film enabled the photographer to see the results in a more 'real world' view, with the inversions of the lens corrected.

The principle for this was actually known before cameras were invented, the system of mirror and prism being used as a drawing aid from as early as the 16th century (often for natural history subjects). The first patented reflex mirror system for a camera was granted in Britain in 1861. Still, the first commercially available SLR was not manufactured and sold until 1884, while it was another half-century until the first mass-market 35mm SLR, Leica's PLOOT reflex housing along with a 200mm f4.5 lens paired to a 35mm rangefinder camera body, made its debut in 1935.

Prior to that landmark innovation, bird photography was already attracting attention.

The July 1906 issue of *National Geographic* (founded 1888) featured the still stunning images (many of birds) of George Shiras III, then in the House of Representatives but who was also an innovative and patient nature photographer, who was even called 'about the most interesting man I know' by Ernest Hemingway.

Shiras was a hunter who put down his guns in 1889, having become more empathetic towards wild animals and birds. He became enamoured with their study and capturing their likenesses, initially with wet plate cameras, but more enthusiastically when he acquired an early hand-held SLR. His restless desire to uncover animals as we never normally see them, by daylight and at night, led him to invent the first flash (called 'flashlight photography' by him), build his own tripwires, be the first to use both canoe and a mobile hide to take photographs, and the first to freeze birds in flight, showing their posture during take-off and in motion.

The 1906 magazine publication saw Shiras achieve almost overnight fame (the issue was reprinted two years later due to demand), and he eventually put together the classic *Hunting Wild Life with Camera and Flashlight* (1935) when his eyesight began to fail him.

Cheaper SLRs like Jhagee's VP Exakta (top) also entered the marketplace in 1935 to compete with Leica, while around the same time self-taught masters of bird photography like Eric Hosking were taking breathtakingly iconic SLR images such as this Barn Owl with prey.

His political career included conservation innovation, and he is one of the congressmen to have helped the Migratory Bird Act through the house in 1916, a forward-thinking piece of legislation ensuring protection for 800 species of bird in the USA and Canada, still in force in modified form today.

The key bird photographer for many British birders was Eric Hosking, and many fans will recall his autobiography *An Eye for a Bird* (1970). However, the Londoner had been photographing wild birds since 1917, when he was eight years old, quietly innovating techniques but remaining unpublished until a Tawny Owl took out his left eye while he climbed to his self-built hide, resulting in national publicity for himself, and inadvertently for his images, too. Many will know his iconic 'Barn Owl with Prey' (1936), and he was the first to use a fast electronic shutter release for flight photography, though he came relatively late to 35mm film in 1963.

Since the 1960s, SLRs have been the camera format of choice for bird photography, being both relatively affordable and practical, offering the benefit of interchangeable lenses and providing top-notch results with practice. The arrival of affordable, high-quality digital SLRs (or DSLRs) since 2003 has exponentially popularised photography among birders.

54 : Kodachrome 35mm film

1936

It is not just the availability of a new technology that can inspire a revolution in popular activity, but also its affordability. Kodachrome 35 mm film was one such innovation, and though eventually outcompeted by even cheaper and more convenient brands, it was probably the most successful commercially sold early colour celluloid still and cinema film.

Developed by the Eastman Kodak Company, the product represented the first retail success of a colour film that used the 'subtractive colour' method still in use today. This technology involved three primary colours being overlaid and absorbing (or subtracting) certain wavelengths to provide a visual representation of the majority of colours that exist in the natural world. This had the advantage of using the actual properties of light rather than the complicated 'additive' mixing of (sometimes counter-intuitive) combinations of coloured inks and dyes that earlier film brands used. The elements of additive colour always became visible on enlargement, and required a large amount of power when used as slide projections owing to their high absorption capacity for light.

Though colour film had existed since the turn of the 20th century, three-colour subtractive Kodachrome was first pushed into the market in 1936 as a 35mm still photography film for professional use, though its price did not prohibit amateurs from also using the product. The film, famed for its fine-grain emulsion, is still regarded as one of the most stable brands in storage. It was initially one of the better slide films (though more specialised products were later developed), and carried the equivalent of approximately 20 megapixels of information in its transparent 24mm x 36mm image. Its complex processing requirements meant that it was sold as 'process-paid' (though this was stopped in the US by a legal ruling in 1954).

This high quality made colour wildlife photography accessible to the hobbyist, opening doors for professionals and the public alike to disseminate their work via widely circulated magazines such as *National Geographic* and, later, *Animals* (now *BBC Wildlife*), as well as in books and exhibitions about the natural world. Kodachrome was even immortalised in the name of a US state park (Utah's Kodachrome Basin SP), as well as a 1973 Paul Simon song.

Always highly regarded but later suffering from stiff competition from the likes of Agfa and Fujichrome, it was the even wider

Widely available and affordable colour film also helped develop
bird photography, enabling detailed images such as these roosting
Dunlins to be taken by the likes of Eric Hosking in 1947.

accessibility and convenience of digital photography that eventually sealed Kodachrome's fate. Production ceased in 2009, with the last colour film being processed in January 2011 before processing chemicals ran out forever. A year later, struggling to cope with the transition from film to digital, Kodak filed for Chapter 11 bankruptcy protection.

55 : Motorola walkie-talkie

1936

Long before mobile phone technology was invented, portable communication devices were limited initially to military use, and Motorola pioneered the 'walkie-talkie', a backpack-carried mobile radio transmitter and receiver, in 1940. This was developed almost simultaneously with the 'handie-talkie' from the same company, and both made a great contribution to the war effort, enabling rapid dissemination of information across both battlefield and training ground.

In the post-war period the devices became more sophisticated and spread into industry and outdoor recreation. Today, walkie-talkies vary considerably in design according to model, function and intended use, but are visually distinguishable from mobile telephones by their push-to-talk and radio channel-selector buttons, lack of an earpiece and fixed antenna. Before mobile phones were so widely available, they fulfilled a key role in spreading news of interesting birds in the field. This practice is well-established in Britain, and Dick Filby of Rare Bird Alert is frequently seen using one to communicate vagrant 'gen' on the Isles of Scilly in the Channel 4 documentary *Birders* (1996).

Elsewhere, though their appeal has remained somewhat limited in birding with the rise of mobile phone technology, many conservation organisations and field workers worldwide use the devices, from African big game reserves to Antarctic research stations, and including the RSPB, which uses handheld radios for both volunteers and staff on some of its larger reserves. In areas where there is little or poor mobile coverage, they can provide a critical – and cost-effective – service, working in the absence of cellular signals and without requiring paid-for connections to other users. Hence they remain popular to this day on Portugal's answer to the Scillies – the Azorean island of Corvo where, each October, Europe's most hardcore listers converge to search for rarities in an impressive volcanic landscape which inhibits mobile phone signals.

Originally developed for the Allied war effort in
1940, walkie-talkies were co-opted by birders to
put out news on hot-spots like Scilly and Fair Isle,
before the advent of mobiles and pagers.

56 : Witherby's *Handbook of British Birds*

1938-41

A giant of his ornithological era, Harry F Witherby's many achievements included the founding of the journal *British Birds* (see pages 96–97) and the British Trust for Ornithology, as well as being awarded an MBE. But no less remarkable was the primary pre-war reference to British birds which he co-authored, the erudite but unwieldy five-volume *The Handbook of British Birds*. He may have shared the credits with the Rev F C R Jourdain, Norman F Ticehurst and Bernard W Tucker, but Britain's first truly comprehensive avifauna was often simply known as 'Witherby', being an expanded version of the editor's earlier two-volume *Practical Handbook of British Birds* (1919-24). Published by Witherby's family publishing firm, *The Handbook* rapidly became the essential ornithological reference work.

Colour and black-and-white plates illustrated virtually all the species recorded in Britain, as well as their nests and eggs, while the complete taxonomic history of all listed forms was given in detail, including every subspecies recorded in Britain. It was also the first one-stop itemisation of all of Britain's rare vagrants, with eye-opening and appetite-whetting foreign gems in every volume. In *British Birds* and these volumes the true roots of the British twitching scene can be found, along with the parochial claiming of 'our' subspecies; debates still go on regarding Scottish Crossbill, Red Grouse and even the 'British' Dartford Warbler.

So illuminating and detailed was the work that it ran to eight impressions, the last being in 1958, as well as a concise edition in 1952 entitled *The Popular Handbook of British Birds*, written by P A D Hollom. A further spin-off in 1960 was *The Popular Handbook of Rarer British Birds*, also by P A D Hollom and featuring the rarest species which had been omitted from the earlier abridged volume.

Ultimately, however, more competition was on the way. The following decade saw the release of the first in the geographically more expansive nine-volume series *Handbook of the Birds of Europe, the Middle East, and North Africa: the Birds of the Western Palearctic*, more simply known as *BWP*. Launched in 1997, this encyclopaedic leviathan eventually superseded *The Handbook*, particularly as birders' eyes were opened by affordable travel to the Continent and awareness of the biogeographical discreteness of their home region.

Further handbooks to the avifaunas of other continents were equally eye-opening, culminating in Lynx Edicions's *The Handbook*

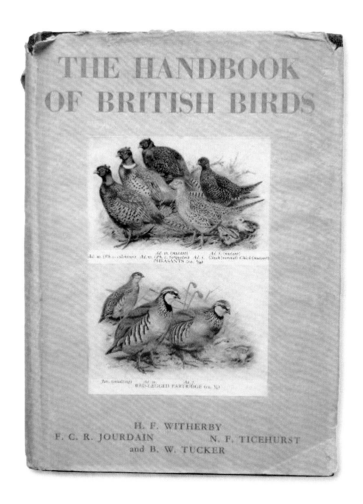

'Witherby' was an ambitious and comprehensive avifauna of Britain, discovered by many a nascent birder in his or her school or public library, and littered throughout with arcane taxonomic and vagrant minutiae – truly the source of the aficionado's attention to detail.

of the Birds of the World which began serial publication in 1992 with the ambitious aim of covering all the world's birds. It is likely to remain the acme of such works, though it is a great investment in book format; *HBW* has been 'reborn' online as a constantly updated database.

Nonetheless, *The Handbook*'s formative inspiration to several generations of birders and ornithologists cannot be underestimated, and there is still fascination and information to be found amidst its fusty minutiae to this day.

57 : *Great Northern?* by Arthur Ransome

1947

Birds are represented comprehensively in literature. Shakespeare's plays allegedly mention hundreds of birds, and Samuel Taylor Coleridge's *Rime of the Ancient Mariner* (1798), John Keats' *Ode to a Nightingale* (1820) and many more poems contribute to the artistic mythology in the same vein. Yet such works don't deal with the perceived need to watch and observe birds. Writers on ornithology and birding themselves are often inspired into flights of lyricism when describing birds and their habitats, perhaps most notably in *The Peregrine* (1967) by J A Baker.

But birders are to a degree under-represented in the creative arts, though particularly since the Second World War their habits and rituals have begun to appear increasingly regularly in movies and in novels. Such appearances say a lot about the public perception of the hobby.

An inspiration for many a growing birder was *Great Northern?* by Arthur Ransome (1947), the final part of his perennially popular *Swallows and Amazons* series of childrens' books. The child heroes of the series try to identify and protect a nesting diver species, against the wishes of an evil egg and specimen collector, and the black-and-white good and evil issues of the book must have stirred many an old-school

conservationist into a lifelong vocation involving birds.

But birding is also represented in other narrative genres. The perceived aloofness of the hobby, often solitary and perhaps the preserve of social misfits, has lent itself well to the crime novel; since the early 1980s, authors such as J S Borthwick, Ann Cleeves, Lydia Adamson and Karen Dudley have added birding to the Agatha Christie via Henning Mankell sweep of the modern crime novel. Cris Freddi has also introduced an existential, Camus-like spin to the genre with *Pelican Blood* (2005), while Sally Hinchcliffe perhaps followed a similar though more original course in her poetic and hypermetaphorical *Out of a Clear Sky* (2009).

Few novelists appear to be genuine birders, but one who may come under that description is the US author Jonathan Franzen, a novelist beloved of Sunday supplements who has become a somewhat self-conscious public face of birding stateside, to the chagrin of some. Authors Margaret Atwood and Graeme Gibson have earned great respect as emissaries and fundraisers for Birdlife International.

Pelican Blood was less successfully adapted to the cinema, while other filmic prejudices of

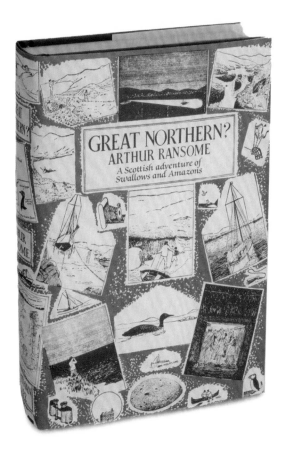

As birding became more widespread as a hobby, birders themselves became figures of eccentricity and caricature in the popular consciousness, subjects sometimes of ridicule, but with the pastime also portrayed as a healthy and suitable occupation for children in novels like *Great Northern?*.

the hobby have been made as artistically poor comedy – step forward *The Big Year* (2011) – and genuinely creepy claustrophobic thriller, in the case of *The Hide* (2008). Aside from repeating essentially the same documentary twice in *Encounters: Birders* (1996) and *Twitchers: A Very British Obsession* (2010), the medium of television once added a surprisingly sympathetic birder to a sitcom in *Watching* (1987-93), a Liverpool-based light comedy which lasted seven series, though the hobby took a quite minor role after the first, mainly being used as a trope, to signify the male lead's shyness and awkwardness.

Birding, therefore, is over-archingly artistically represented as the pastime of stalkers, murderers, deceivers and cuckolds, with only the protagonist of an Eighties sitcom approaching the more mundane reality – a far cry from Arthur Ransome's 1947 portrayal. The motivations, excitements and passions of the hobby – in fact, the birds themselves – are still seemingly a mystery to most writers and the general public.

58 : Questar telescope

1954

Most wild birds are innately wary, so the problem for anyone who wants to watch or study them in detail is how to do so without disturbance. Skills developed through hunting, such as stalking or hiding, can sometimes be usefully deployed, but the ideal way to get close to a suspicious or unco-operative bird is to do it with magnifying optics. While binoculars have a long and important history in this respect (see pages 88–89), the practical limitations of magnification for a hand-held instrument mean that in birding situations, a telescope is frequently the best option.

'Scopes' have a considerable history, dating back to the first revelatory and revolutionary uses of lenses to bring objects closer, and birds were almost the first objects to be viewed through an arrangement of consecutive lenses in a cylinder. Primitive quartz lenses are known from prehistory, and were used for reading and starting fires by the 12th century.

Corrective concave lenses were being combined in a frame as spectacles by the late 1400s, but the idea for placing both a concave and convex lens together to see over a distance is generally attributed to a letter written by Giambattista della Porta in 1586.

The first telescopes had been invented in The Netherlands by 1608, collecting visible light through simple glass lenses and mirrors. The invention is attributed variously to Hans Lippershey, Sacharius Jansen (both spectacle makers) or Jacob Metius, and Lippershey's at least was capable of a 3x magnification or so. Possibly apocryphally, it is told that Lippershey's children used two of his lenses in tandem to look at birds nesting under a church spire, thus effectively using them for birding before astronomy, and inspiring him to mount them in a tube. News of this discovery had reached Galileo by 1609, and he was already developing the device for astronomical use only one year after that.

It wasn't until the 20th century that the instrument diverged into the many forms known today. Originally intended for the amateur astronomer, the Questar 3.5" was the first commercially available compact telescope, though far from affordable, and was soon used for watching wildlife after its introduction in 1954. The Questar Birder model appeared just a few years later, with an angled eyepiece and magnifications of 40x and 160x.

Initially its use was difficult, as, along with the wind-wobble expected at high magnifications, the image was counter-intuitively reversed, meaning that a bird moving from left to right would appear to be moving in the opposite direction through the scope. Its appearance has remained pretty much the same since it first hit the market.

Questar models were beyond most birders' budgets, and the most popular affordable

It didn't take birders who had been in the armed forces long to adapt the optics
of warfare to finding and bringing birds within closer range, but Questar was
the first company to develop a telescope specifically for the hobby.

scopes were probably Broadhurst Clarkson brass draw-tube models, initially designed for military use in the 19th century and representing good value for clarity and brightness. The Mark I to Mark VI were introduced until just after the Second World War, and came in their own fetching 'boy scout' brown leather protective case, had a 5cm aperture, 7.5cm sunscreens at the end, and could be extended up to 80cm in some models, with a top magnification of 40x.

This sounds good, but telescopes with the nature watcher/hunter in mind had been manufactured since the late 19th century with magnifications up to at least 40x, though quality was minimal. Brass telescopes are still on sale today, mostly for the astronomy and ornamental markets.

The beginning of the 1970s saw basic draw-tube, naval-style scopes superseded by the fixed-length Supra made by Nickel AG, a company best known for its hunting scopes and rifle sights. As such models were adopted by

birders, the money to be made from this emerging market was becoming apparent, and there was soon a preponderance of high-end choice which has continued to increase to this day. Tripods and car mounts were already in use (see pages 182–183), the former from photography and the latter from hunting.

Angled eyepieces were an early innovation during this expansion, to enable taller birders get a comfortable view, minimise wind vibration at a lower tripod setting or for detailed notes and sketches to be made without taking an eye off the bird. Interchangeable eyepieces also took off, allowing zoom and wide-angle usage as well as the more usual fixed magnification. Far from being limited to a co-opted astronomical scope, birders could make purchases according to specialised field requirements, taste and budget. The growing popularity of birdwatching saw most optics companies enter the market, and as identification skills have become more forensic, higher-quality telescopes are in great demand.

59 : Mass spectrometer

1958

The technique of mass spectrometry is a method of showing the masses of molecules in a material using a graphic technique to represent the distribution of their ions. In other words, the proportions and types of elements present can be displayed as a graph on paper. The method was first applied to the proteins of animals in 1958 by Carl-Ove Andersson, a Swede.

Its application in birding may seem obscure at first, but the technique has actually been used to partially settle one of birding's oldest conundrums – that of the origin of rare or exotic wildfowl. Birders, and perhaps more critically records committees, are loathe to 'count' a potentially vagrant duck or goose owing to the familiar worldwide practice of keeping imported wildfowl in captivity in large numbers, frequently breeding them (and almost as frequently hybridising them).

Isotope-ratio mass spectrometry (IRMS) is the precise term for the forensic technique in which the relative abundance of isotopes can be detected by vapourising a sample of organic material; this can indicate the geographic origin of a sample by its chemical constituents, normally only locating its source to a major geological or pedological zone. In the case of a

putatively vagrant duck, isotopes of the commonly occurring element will show a proportion that correlates with that of the local precipitation in the region where its feathers were grown. Moult timing means that retained juvenile feathers will provide good samples of isotopes derived from a breeding site, indicating an individual's natal origin. Migrant first-winter birds are thus an ideal source of samples.

The origin of individual migratory birds can, therefore, be inferred from these isotopes, as in some cases can their wintering grounds. From a birding perspective, the anticipated vagrancy potential of a species can actually be proved in some cases. Baikal Teal, an east Asian duck, has been added to the British list on the basis of a first-winter individual shot in Denmark in November 2005; analysis demonstrated that the Danish bird was a genuine vagrant via the stable-hydrogen isotope characteristics of a Siberian origin in its juvenile feathers, contrasting with adult feathers containing an isotope ratio more typical of the Atlantic European environment in which it was found. Clearly, in simple terms, if wild Baikal Teal can make it all the way to Denmark, they can reach Britain too. A

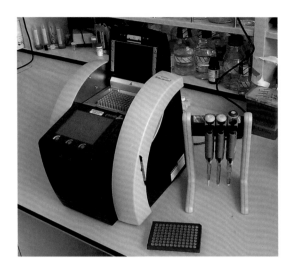

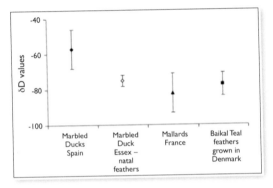

Mass spectrometry (top) is part of the forensic and detective armoury
that more and more birders seem to expect to answer their questions
about what they can actually count on their lists of sightings.
Sometimes the answer is disappointing, as when a Marbled Duck
(above right) shot in Essex turned out to be a likely escapee.

British-shot Baikal Teal (from 2006) has also
been tested with the same results.

However, it isn't all good news: the same
isotopes tested from the feathers of a 2007
Essex-shot Marbled Duck – viewed by a
majority of British birders as a highly feasible
rare vagrant – showed it to have little chemical
difference in its juvenile and adult feathers,
and was most likely to have been raised on the
northern European coast, indicating a captive
origin away from its natural Mediterranean
and Middle Eastern breeding sites. A Falcated
Duck specimen taken on Shapinsay, Orkney, in
November 2000 is still undergoing tests in the
hope of proving the species' natural vagrancy
potential to British birders.

60 : Sonogram

1958

What birders know as a sonogram is more properly called a spectrogram, and is a visual representation of the full frequency spectrum of a particular sound or series of sounds – in this instance the songs and calls of birds.

Usually illustrated as a black-and-white, two-dimensional graph-like figure, visual renderings of a sound source can be remarkably informative once one is used to reading them while listening to the original source – almost like reading music – and can be a great aid when analysing and comparing avian vocalisations.

The visual study of sound in fact dates back to 1857, when Édouard-Léon Scott de Martinville invented the phonautograph, which was in fact the first device that could record sound waves. Built to solely enable the visual study of recorded sound, no playback was possible, but the sound waves were inscribed onto a rotating cylinder of soot-coated paper by a needle or stylus. The stylus traced a line through the soot which represented the motions of a diaphragm or membrane that physically responded to the sounds via a series of levers.

Sonograms tend to be graphically represented by axes, just like a histogram or graph: the x- or horizontal axis represents time, and the y- or vertical axis the frequency, usually measured in kilohertz (khz). Though often printed in monochrome, colour versions can also be produced and these are arguably richer in timbral information.

Bird sounds were first analysed in this way in an *Ibis* paper on the songs of two Chaffinch subspecies by W H Thorpe in 1958, entitled 'The learning of song patterns by birds, with especial reference to the song of the Chaffinch *Fringilla coelebs*'. The format has become very prevalent in birding circles in the last decade, particularly so now that the idea that song or calls can reproductively isolate populations enough to create new species has taken hold in the birding consciousness.

However, in the rush to try and claim new species, it is sometimes forgotten that calls and songs can be merely dialects or local variations, that vocalisations are also 'plastic' and learnt, and that true reproductive isolation involves more than just geography and minor variations in mating sounds, but also subtly complex differences in behaviour and actual insurmountable physiological and morphological change.

The sonogram itself is, however, a valuable

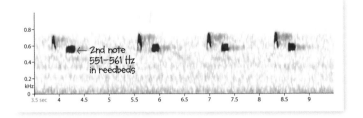

← 2nd note
551–561 Hz
in reedbeds

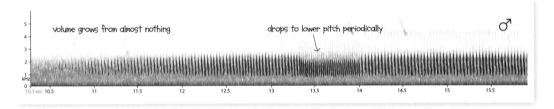

volume grows from almost nothing   drops to lower pitch periodically   ♂

With experience, sonograms for Common Cuckoo (top, pictured left) and
European Nightjar (above, pictured right) can actually be read in almost the
same way as musical notation, as they show both pitch and timbre to a degree.

analytical tool for all students of bird vocalisations, amateur and professional, and relatively easy to understand for most birders once they take the plunge. Production and analysis is neither a specialist nor expensive business – several free downloadable programs, including Raven Lite from Cornell Laboratory of Ornithology, are now available for any birder with a computer to produce their own sonograms from their own recordings (or others), and there are even smartphone apps to perform similar tasks. The study and interpretation of bird sounds has been taken to extraordinary new levels by The Sound Approach, a pioneering group whose analysis of chosen subjects has, among other things, led to the 'splitting' of new storm-petrel species and the discovery in Oman of an owl new to science.

61 : Swoop wild bird food

c. 1958

People have at least casually fed those bird species that became commensal or habituated to human settlements as far back as ancient Egypt, but the earliest recorded incident of intentional bird feeding appears to be that of Saint Serf, who lived in Fife, Scotland, from c.500 to 583 AD. In more recent times, harsh winters at the end of the 19th century saw newspapers and magazines encouraging the feeding of wild birds, and in the 20th century it became a national pastime.

Kitchen scraps and stale bread aside, the commercial prospects of selling foods manufactured specifically for wild birds became truly apparent in late 1940s America, when the Wagner Brothers Feed Company and Knauf & Tesch collaborated on combining their animal and pet food products to create a market for commercial bird food. Capitalising on the post-war growth in suburban living, they inspired many proud owners of back yards to begin putting food out for birds.

In late 1950s Britain, the launch of a brand of bird seed called Swoop soon cornered the domestic market for the ensuing decade. By the 1970s, it was on sale in most pet shops for around 25 new pence, its popularity increased by possibly the first appearance of Bill Oddie

in a bird product advert. Swoop contained around a dozen species of weed seed imported from the Near East and North Africa, many of which then grew as exotic aliens in English gardens. The mix included sunflower, millet, wheat, flakes of maize, hemp, peanuts, linseed, barley and many weed seeds inadvertently included as part of the same harvests.

The popularity of the product was later eclipsed by the RSPB and other pet shop brands, which began providing fat and suet balls, seed mixes intended for different groups of birds, and latterly Nyger seed for smaller seed-eating finches such as Siskin and Goldfinch in particular. Many cage and aviary bird seed suppliers, notably Haith's, quickly began producing wild bird mixes and became market leaders, while a good number of farms such as Vine House Farm now grow crops solely for the purpose of providing seed mixes for wild birds. The last decade has seen a continuing expansion of this market into major supermarkets and garden centres, and even the widespread option of a bulk-buy pick'n'mix-type selection from large tubs at many RSPB reserves.

Such a simple and direct product and market relationship has surprisingly harboured

Swoop wild bird food provided a varied selection of seeds
to attract wild birds such as Blue Tits to gardens, and being
available through the rapidly expanding supermarkets also
brought the notion of feeding birds to public attention.

scandal recently, when US company Scotts
Miracle-Gro was fined $4.5 million in 2012
for knowingly supplying 73 million packets of
wild bird seed contaminated with dangerous
pesticides, of which they were only able to
recall two million in time to prevent them
from being used. It is impossible to know how
many birds were killed by this huge quantity of
poisoned seed, but a San Diego couple who fed
the product to almost 100 aviary birds in
January 2010 were left with a mere eight
individuals shortly after.

62 : Tiger Tops

1964

As the world opened up to independent and package travellers, and wildlife documentaries and books encouraged a fascination with animals and exotica, so the public increasingly wanted to see such exciting and foreign places – and their wildlife – for themselves. Few, however, wanted to endure the hardship of the explorers that first discovered these places for western eyes. Many were far removed from 'mod cons' or even what the moneyed travellers of the mid-20th century middle class would call basic accommodation.

Chitwan National Park in Nepal was one of the first of the truly exotic reserves to gain international attention, being featured in several early documentaries and containing such charismatic creatures as Leopard, Sloth Bear, Indian Rhinoceros and Bengal Tiger. This last beast gave its name to two lodges at the park, Tiger Tops, the first of which was constructed in 1964 to house customers for the owners' Nepal Wildlife Adventures in up to 22 rooms.

Compatibility with conservation was always paramount, and, and what was effectively the first 'ecolodge' sourced local produce and employed local people from the outset, in collaboration with the Smithsonian Institution in the United States. Such places frequently attracted wealthier birders, and so they could be said to contribute a substantial amount to local communities that otherwise might value their natural assets for merely exploitative reasons.

Ecolodges are now found in most important wildlife areas around the globe, and making wildlife available for the leisure and pleasure of the nature-oriented is possibly the most important part of declaring and protecting a national park. Most NP-designated reserves are full of, and sometimes explicitly created for, birds, and lodges like Cocha Cashu Biological Station at Manu National Park in Peru have an impressive list of 500 or more bird species available within hiking distance of the facilities.

In essence, a national park was defined in 1969 by the International Union for the Conservation of Nature (IUCN) as a minimum 1,000-ha area covering several ecosystems unaltered by human activities and containing animals and plants of special scientific interest. Once declared, it must be protected by the highest authority of the government concerned, and staff and finance must be provided to maintain the integrity of parks, with economically essential visiting allowed for educational and recreational reasons. Birders combine both, of course, and continue to be disproportionately influential in establishing and investigating the major habitats of the globe.

Tiger Tops in Chitwan National Park, Nepal, was the first of many
ecolodges that opened up in nature reserves around the globe to cater
for the burgeoning ranks of ecotourists and world birdwatchers.

63 : Dictaphone Travel-Master

1965

While most birders in the Sixties opted to transcribe their notes and observations in time-honoured fashion in notebooks and journals, another option emerged entirely by chance. Though it was never widely adopted, a minority embraced the technology of the touch-typist to keep 'live' *aides memoire*, using a Dictaphone.

Though the trade name had been around since 1907, the first compact and portable tape recorder under the name was released in 1947. But it was another 18 years until the most popular model, the Dictaphone Travel-Master, was launched. First issued in 1965, it could be powered by batteries and record up to an hour's worth of 'notes' – perfect for use in the field.

Other small portable machines were produced by Philips, using full-sized standard blank music cassettes, and Olympus, which opted for micro-cassettes, themselves also adapted for telephone answering machines (see pages 92–93). Dictaphone answered its rivals by developing the Pico cassette for the dictation industry, enabling the company to reduce the size of its recorders in turn.

Through the 1970s, music tape recorders and players were also diminishing in size, and the most popular and famous of these was released onto the market by Sony in 1979: The Walkman. The machine was small enough to be fitted into a jacket pocket or even attached to a belt, and also came kitted out with headphones and microphones. The brand dominated the mobile music retail scene of the 1980s, powered by cheap alkaline batteries and a burgeoning cassette market. The best quality machine was the Walkman Professional, introduced in 1982, which became frequently used by amateur wildlife sound recordists.

The advent of digital recording in the 1990s saw the Walkman gradually eclipsed by the MiniDisc, another Sony innovation launched in 1992 which could hold up to 80 minutes of recorded data (equivalent to a CD in sound terms). The recording quality was not as good as a CD, and that clarity of reproduction awaited the later introduction of linear PCM (pulse-code modulation) digital recording. MiniDiscs ceased production in March 2013.

Digital voice recorders were launched in 1991 and survive to this day, being able to record up to eight hours of sound on several different tracks, and possessing most of the other benefits of modern recording such as instant rewind and fast forward, and the marking of tracks for later reference.

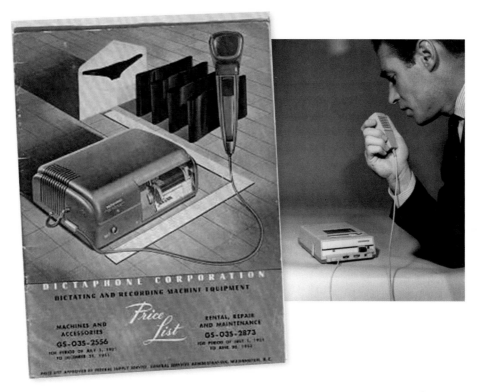

Some birders used Dictaphones and similar devices to keep track of their sightings, writing their observations up later in logs and journals. Subsequently, digital voice recording, especially on mobile phones, replaced tape-based machines.

All these devices have been used for oral note-taking by birders, usually being written up as hard copy when the user gets home. But all have now been eclipsed by mobile phones, which can record several hours of voice and even bird song for storage, download, editing or transcription. However, joint 'old school' portable dictation and bird sound recording partly lives on in the form of a 21st century invention, Remembird. This novel device attaches between the two barrels of a binocular, and the small microphone inside it records the sounds of the bird under observation, as well as

the user's own 'of the moment' commentary, if desired. Remembird has a 'rolling' recording method – in which everything is recorded while watching, and retained for eight seconds before the recording is triggered – a close 'mic' for spoken observations and an audio field guide for many regions of the globe.

Despite its nifty convenience and novel design, Remembird will no longer be manufactured and company support will stop in 2015, making the device perhaps another victim of the rapidly evolving digital revolution.

64 : Super 8

1965

Capturing scenes of life on film is a way of preserving the moment, reliving it at any time in the future and keeping the details of memory clear. The invention of 35mm celluloid movie film (essentially the same as still camera film) spawned what has been termed 'the art form of the 20th century' by film director Martin Scorsese, and enabled the first appearances of wild birds at the cinema and later on television.

Fred Ott Holding a Bird (William Dickson, 1894) is probably the first appearance of a bird in a motion picture, the silent, black-and-white 35mm short being one of the earliest surviving movies. It was viewed by audiences on kinetoscopes, on which individuals viewed the flickering, jerky pictures on standalone boxes with a peephole.

Movie cameras were already portable enough by 1923 to be taken on the Tanager Expedition to the northernmost Hawaiian Islands, where groundbreaking ornithologist Alexander Wetmore was able to take the last ever footage of Laysan Rail before it disappeared forever, after only having been discovered in abundance on Midway and Laysan fewer than 100 years before. This ability to preserve lost species for all time is doubly highlighted by the

film taken of Ivory-billed Woodpecker in 1935 by P P Kellogg; this invaluable sequence also has sound recordings. A notable failure of the 21st century claim of the rediscovery of this extinct bird was the film produced by scientists as 'evidence', but which actually apparently showed a Pileated Woodpecker (see pages 166-167).

It was the production of cheap and practical 8mm film and cameras that enabled people to make their own home movies, and a number of birdwatchers were quick to use the format for their own ends to record sightings and birding trips. The Standard 8 format was first released onto the market in 1932 by the ever-innovatory Eastman Kodak, though the film itself was actually 16mm wide, despite the name. The film enabled images to be captured along one 8mm side, before being flipped and recording taking place on the other. 16mm was also used in the field, notably for shooting the last footage of Imperial Woodpecker in Mexico on a Cornell University expedition in 1956.

Sales really burgeoned in 1965 with the introduction of the Super 8 format, which used easily loadable and cheaply developed cartridges for its films. Magnetic soundtrack tape was added to the edge of some later

Filming birds is ultimately the most accurate way of recording their
movements and behaviour, no matter how good an artist or
note-taker you are, and Super 8 cameras offered a portable means
of recording rarities and birding trips, though digital technology
would take this to a whole new level.

products but didn't really catch on, though the original format is still used today by a small number of amateur filmmakers, being transferred or telecined onto video tape in the production process.

The reduction in bulk and weight of 8mm equipment started a trend that came of age with home video, a medium that really helped the everyday birder begin to record sightings as home movies, and immeasurable lengths of old footage of birds almost certainly now languish in unformatted purgatory.

65 : YOC badge

1965

How to get young people interested in natural history, and specifically birding, is a perennial question, and the RSPB had an answer – actually, several answers – in its youth division. Originally this took the form of the Junior Bird Recorders' Club, launched in 1943, but with much greater appeal and more influential to the current generation of middle-aged birders was the Young Ornithologists' Club (YOC), which replaced it in 1965 and flourished until 2000.

Local YOC groups were particularly successful in schools and on dedicated field courses, where many budding birders went on their first trips to visit nature reserves and have their first sightings of species that hitherto had only been known from the few bird books in the school or local library. At its peak in 1980 YOC membership topped 100,000, its budding young members reading their *Bird Life* magazines enthusiastically and wearing their hovering Kestrel badges with pride.

Lifelong friendships were forged, careers and hobbies inspired, and tips and experiences exchanged, and many schoolchildren who did not become or remain birders retained enough interest in wildlife to maintain memberships of wildlife and conservation charities, feed their garden birds and perhaps even consider green policies of importance in political parties' manifestos.

At the turn of the century, the YOC was succeeded by the Wildlife Explorers – a broad-brush evolution of the earlier clubs aimed at children aged eight to 12, and currently with more than 170,00 members. Additionally, RSPB Phoenix was launched for teenagers in 1995, and now boasts more than 38,000 members. Both encourage field trips and volunteering, and both have house magazines in *Wild Times* and *Bird Life* respectively.

Conservationists have become ever more conscious of the disconnection of young people from the natural world, perhaps as most now have children and have noticed the differences in lifestyle from their own at the same age. This concern came to a head with the publication of the National Trust's *Natural Childhood* report (2012), written by TV producer and naturalist Stephen Moss. Many experts

"Give me the child, and I will mould the man," a Jesuit missionary is alleged to have said. Birding charities and organisations have taken a more innocent version of this maxim to mind, continually creating initiatives and clubs to encourage young birders, including perhaps the most successful: the RSPB's Young Ornithologists' Club.

and organisations were consulted on their thoughts about the public in general and children in particular being out of touch with nature, though there was little agreement about what could be done.

With membership of the RSPB's youth organisations healthy, the many other children who are not experiencing wild animals and natural habitats can perhaps be encouraged by school trips and the greening of urban areas. The future is up for grabs, and *Natural Childhood* may help us enter it not entirely blindly.

66 : *Where to Watch Birds* by John Gooders

1967

Many birders will remember that after they first took up their binoculars and became familiar with the birds of their local area, or perhaps after a Young Ornithologists' Club trip to an accessible RSPB reserve, branching out further afield was reliant on the recommendations of the more experienced or on word of mouth from other birders.

This was to change in 1967 when John Gooders, a teacher originally from south London, produced the then revolutionary *Where to Watch Birds*, a comprehensive new-format directory of Britain's best birdwatching sites. The Rosetta Stone of birding travel guides, it would be the trigger for countless journeys to often little-known but ornithologically productive locations around the country. Many thousand of copies of the various editions of this horizon-broadening volume were sold, and by 1970 the follow-up *Where to Watch Birds in Britain and Europe* was also proving popular as package tours and the first wildlife-oriented holidays boosted birders' tastes for the exotic.

Gooders's books held their own for the greater part of two decades, although later editions of the European volume somewhat surreally included destinations such as Israel

and The Gambia on the spurious basis that they were often visited by British birders. This was an unwitting admission that the reachable world was becoming ever larger, and that the demand for more globe-trotting information had outgrown the material supplied by the two original *Where to Watch Birds* volumes.

Beyond the boundaries of Europe, it often wasn't widely known where the best places to see birds were, and the difficulties of access, season, language and other complications needed elucidating. Birders' personal trip reports, photocopied and passed on, provided more practical bird-finding advice in this respect; before long, this basic but effective format was adopted by the enterprising Dave Gosney for his first Gostours guides. Initially little more than pamphlets, they were typed, illustrated with self-drawn maps and cheaply reproduced to good effect, recounting personal experiences at each site covered and often pinpointing exactly where, when and how key target species could be seen in a range of destinations.

Others developed the site guide genre still further, and none more so than Christopher Helm. From the late Eighties, the publisher rolled out guide after guide covering English

Knowledge of Britain's best birding sites was almost a state secret before the publication of 'Gooders', which encouraged a whole generation to fully explore the country's wild places and seek out its birds.

regions, Scotland, Wales and Ireland, and ultimately almost every continent. With updated editions of the domestic titles often appearing at regular intervals, many of the guides remain essential companions on independent birding ventures. Other publishers including Prion, the American Birding Association and, latterly, Crossbill Guides, as well as a wide range of independents, continue to specialise in detailing birdwatching areas not well covered elsewhere.

Like all facets of the hobby, however, these books are undergoing a serious challenge from the free, easily accessible, partisan and up-to-the-minute information available online on forums, websites and newsgroups, much of which is now becoming available in the field to the owners of smartphones, tablets and laptops. But the advent of ebooks and by extension a new digital lease of life for the original guides may yet ensure a future for the professionally written and published legacy of the original 'Gooders'.

67 : Gore-Tex

1969

The problem of what to wear outdoors is one that birders know only too well – man-made fibres cause undue perspiration, while natural fibres are too porous and permeable. This becomes more of a problem the tougher the environment, and as birders pursue their quarry in difficult terrain and unfamiliar climates, clothing ascends the priority list. Wouldn't it be great if there was a fabric that was as waterproof as nylon but as breathable as cotton?

Well there almost is, and its inventor, Robert Gore, was ensconced into no less than the US National Inventors Hall of Fame because of it.

In 1969 Gore was able to produce an expanded polytetrafluoroethylene (ePTFE), or Gore-Tex to give it his commercial name, providing an affordable way to manufacture outdoor clothing that let water vapour pass from the inside but prevented precipitation from entering. ePTFE is virtually the same as

Teflon, the familiar coating of non-stick cooking pans, and when layered with nylon and polyurethane to give it support and strength, the fabric is able to effectively, though not absolutely perfectly, control water entry and exit from a garment.

Though fairly universal among outdoor outer garments today, the material's introduction was not without controversy. Only a year after its first use in 1969, Gore had to sue Garlock, Inc, for patent infringement, though this has not stopped the production of several other materials using similar principles and chemicals since.

Repeated wear often reduces the effectiveness of Gore-Tex's water repellent covering, which can be something of an Achilles heel, but nonetheless many birders, explorers, hunters and hikers owe much of the dryness and warmth of their bodies and feet in the lonely wilderness to Gore and his ingenious fabric.

Practical and portable outdoor clothing (above, middle) was given a real boost by Bob Gore's (top) Gore-Tex technology (bottom), paving the way for today's birder- and naturalist-specific brands like Country Innovation and Páramo.

68 : Nancy's Café

1970s

Rare bird news may be widely and instantly available these days, but it wasn't always that way. Before the modern era of rapid dissemination of sightings via mobiles, pagers and the web, it wasn't a question of 'what you knew' so much as 'who you knew'. Connecting with the right people was critical to success if you were in the business of 'ticking' rarities, and the grapevine that linked those involved was centred on a simple eatery on the A149 in Norfolk: Nancy's Café at Cley-next-the-Sea.

As one of the country's top birding spots, the marshes at Cley – once the local patch of celebrated bird artist R A Richardson – attracted many birders to the area as well as birds. The village became something of a social hub as well as a leading reserve, and a hardcore nucleus of birders, many well-known names of the day among them, adopted Nancy's Café as a home from home.

Nancy's was owned and run by the appropriately named Nancy and Jack Gull, operating from their own dining room. They employed locals, served cheap fry-ups and other home-made food, and provided a meeting place for most of Britain's keenest birders, and especially the first generation of twitchers. The communal *laissez faire* and

tolerant atmosphere of the café in its prime (it closed in December 1988, with eulogies in the national media) has been well captured in Mark Cocker's classic birdwatching memoir, *Birders: Tales of a Tribe* (2002). It was the place to be for many, though it also had the capacity to seem cliquey to some, especially newcomers to birding.

From a modern perspective, the 'news service' available through Nancy's Café was rudimentary at best. Birders from around the country would call the widely known phone number and ask the oft-repeated question of the day, 'Anything about?'. A diary by the phone would detail the news, local and national, which – assuming the phone was answered (typically by a birding customer rather than by staff) – would then be read out to the caller. In peak periods, the person sitting closest to the phone would struggle to eat a meal while it was hot. News from elsewhere would also be received and added to the list of rarity sightings already in the book. As a system it worked well enough in its own way, but the limitations were obvious.

Nancy's true significance, apart from helping ardent listers connect with new birds, was as the launch pad for Birdline, the service

Nancy's Café was legendary among the twitching fraternity, with infamous bread pudding and beans on toast being served by familiar staff like Ethel the waitress; those days were caricatured by Bill Morton in spoof birding magazine, *Not BB*.

that took over the mantle for providing rare bird news. Also Norfolk-based, it began life as an answering machine in the warden's hut at Walsey Hills NNT reserve just east of Cley. Warden Roy Robinson would record a message and update it as and when work, time and news permitted. Then came a rival network in the shape of the Bird Information Service, also based at Cley and launched by Richard Millington and Steve Gantlett. Before long the two operations became one, and the enterprise expanded with the introduction of premium rate phone lines.

Three decades later Birdline still provides a rare bird news service, as do its regional franchises. Though the popularity of phone-based services has waned, most birders active since the 1980s will at some point have found themselves in a phone box with a pile of coins trying to get news of the latest national rarities – a practice that can be traced directly back to Nancy Gull and her much-loved village café.

69 : Hand-held mobile phone

1973

So ubiquitous are mobile phones in the modern era that it is hard to imagine ever birding without one. Not only are they essential for rapid dissemination of sightings via call, text or social media, but also for a variety of other tasks in the field, from 'phonescoping' still images or video to playing bird songs and calls on apps, or even recording them with in-built microphones.

Such impressive technological achievements are, of course, relatively recent. They certainly weren't apparent when John Mitchell and Dr Martin Cooper of Motorola demonstrated their first 1kg mobile handset in 1973. Remarkably, however, long before then devices containing at least a good part of the modern concept had been conceived. As early as 1906 Charles Alden invented a 'vest pocket telephone', while 40 years later a limited car phone and 3-32 channel, three-bandwidth phone systems were in operation, though they were extremely unwieldy and localised within the USA.

The first commercially available mobiles were the size of a house brick, retailed at almost $4,000 and used regular public phonelines; the first public network was opened in Japan in 1979. Product evolution was slow at first, but handsets a decade later were already a vast improvement. The addition of text messaging in 1992 caused a real revolution, enabling much cheaper personal communication.

Mobile phones are now no longer the luxury preserve of the first world, having really taken off in developing countries, where few had access to phones before the advent of cheap and often disposable handsets. But with popularity there are problems: the huge amounts of data used worldwide in mobile telephony cannot continue to expand indefinitely. Modern smartphones produce 35 times the data traffic that the average 'cellphone' used to generate, and the amount of bandwidth available is finite. Industry pundits are expecting bandwidth to be full by 2016 in some western countries, when usage is expected to be 60 times greater than it was 2012.

In the meantime, the popularity of mobile phones in birding will continue to surge as more and more useful apps are launched, in-phone cameras are improved and social media finds new ways to connect birders with each other.

Martin Cooper, inventor of what became known by many as 'the brick' – mobiles rapidly became much more compact, and with improved battery life became almost essential in the field for many.

70 : Petzl head lamp

1973

Night birding is a very niche sub-hobby, but essential should one wish to see the behaviour of those aerial insect specialists the nightjars, witness many many of the hunting techniques of owls or study nocturnally active nesting seabirds. Like so many forms of birding, the equipment required is a bastardisation of gear from other hobbies, in this case caving, with – as also often happens – input from the military.

Head lamps were developed by the caving company Petzl in 1973 to enable hands-free exploration of dark places, and these soon became used for backpackers and campers to find their way around in the dark. Both uses are also now prevalent among birders when the need arises. Of course, torches have existed for a long time, but a head lamp's ease of use keeps hands available for binoculars (which are often usable at dusk nowadays), as well as for holding on to trees and rocks in difficult terrain.

LED lighting has been a recent technological advance applied to the traditional battery-powered flashlight and now also to head lamps, enabling distinctly protracted use. This is particularly advantageous when away from an electricity or battery source for days, as many world birders are. White light emitting diodes, as they are properly known, are also less fragile than the glass bulbs used in most household torches. The best head lamps use a number of LEDs for differing levels of illumination and colour (red light being preferable to white in situations where birds might otherwise be attracted to the light).

Though available since the Second World War, goggles, monoculars and binoculars designed for night vision are rarely used by birders, partly because of cost but also because their low resolution and magnification generally restricts their usefulness to watching large animals. However, this technology is developing all the time and a more appropriate use may become apparent in the future.

Though not strictly for birding use, head lamps have
proved invaluable for long birding trips involving
camping, being used to find one's way at night or
reading when there is no other light source.

71 : Radio tag

1973

Ringing is reliant on refinding marked birds, which have average recovery rates of less than 0.18 per cent. This fact alone means that huge numbers have to be ringed for any statistically meaningful result to emerge. Radio and satellite transmitters have changed all that by enabling individual birds to be tracked constantly throughout their travels – probably the most revelatory technological breakthrough in ornithology.

Tagging techniques, also known as telemetry, evolved from military use in the USA in the mid-20th century. The technology was first deployed in wildlife research in the early 1960s. The first radio frequency identification device (RFID) was patented by Mario Cardullo in 1973, and enabled individuals to be identified and tracked.

The techniques have been highly useful in determining migration strategies, habitat use, population levels, intra- and inter-specific relationships and survival capability. Spatial tracking methods include VHF (Very High Frequency) radio tracking, Ultra High Frequency (UHF) wavelengths and GPS (Global Positioning System) technologies on miniature Platform Transmitter Terminals (PTTs), battery-powered and carried by the bird. GPS locates devices to within a few metres by triangulating signals from three or four different satellites. Positional data can be stored in the digital memory of some devices or sent directly to a receiver or computer.

Cost and effectiveness mean that bird-tracking schemes are often funded by governments, for instance during the 'bird flu' scare, when satellite tagging was used to uncover possible H5N1 virus transport routes. Whooper Swans migrating from Russia to eastern Asia were expected to show a pattern comparable to the dispersal route of the virus, but tag signals showed their patterns and timings to be different. The human-contractable form of the disease was thus found to be more likely spread via the commercial movement of poultry from east to west by European factory farms.

The technique also has great conservation importance. The critically endangered Siberian Crane has had important stop-over sites in China on the way to its main wintering site of Poyang Lake identified by tagging, marked birds helping locate areas where resources and strategies needed to be implemented the most.

The distance, endurance, speed and survival

Radio tags provide highly individual and intimate
insights into the rovings of birds, such as this young Red
Kite (main photo); as the technology evolves, the size of
the transmitters continually decreases (inset).

abilities of birds have been well illuminated.
Bar-tailed Godwits fly south from Alaska to
winter in New Zealand and Australasia,
travelling up to 7,258 miles almost non-stop
over a nine-day trans-Pacific journey. On its
hitherto poorly known migration, the secretive
Great Snipe has been logged at an average
ground speed of almost 56mph travelling from
northern Sweden to tropical central Africa.

When a Hungarian-tagged Saker Falcon was
tracked to Spain and then Mauritania before it
was found dead, the species' previously
unknown wanderings – and therefore vagrancy
potential to Britain – were confirmed, as were
the dangers in dispersal and the necessity for
cross-border conservation initiatives. Another
raptor, a wayward European Honey-buzzard,
was tragically tracked on computer screens as it
attempted to migrate south-west from Britain,
only for the signal to disappear in the Atlantic.

Perhaps the most publicly popular satellite-
tracking scheme to date is the BTO's Cuckoo
Tracking Project begun in 2011, where
'sponsored' Common Cuckoos are followed as
they migrate to and from tropical African
wintering grounds. Again, through this
technology new routes were illustrated, as were
the dangers facing long-distance migrants – by
spring 2013, only four out of the original 19
young birds survived.

The technology is being constantly refined.
Reduction in transmitter size is the way
forward, preventing discomfort to the birds.
The Avian NanoTag can weigh as little as
0.29g, measure 11mm and last several months;
hundreds of birds can be assigned to one
frequency, with individual details retained.

Clearly, as the technology gets smaller, more
powerful and less expensive, new revelations
can only continue to be forthcoming.

72 : *Seventy Years of Birdwatching* by H G Alexander

1974

Whether as a constantly evolving hobby or a multi-faceted vocation, a fascination with birds is often lifelong. Consequently, many aficionados lead interesting lives, to say the least. The fact that so many contribute to reports, journals, magazines and books, and are well travelled with a wealth of resulting material, means that towards the end of their lives the desire to put experiences down on paper can be irresistible.

The birding memoir has become a genre unto itself, and it's difficult to label any particular book as the first, due to the prevalence of ornithological and biological biographies in the 19th century and even before. In fact, a life dedicated to the study or observation of animals and birds will make for an eventful journey, in both a literal and a metaphorical sense. For instance, Henry Seebohm (of courser and wheatear fame) wrote the posthumously printed two-volume *Birds of Siberia* (1901), a classic of privation and hardship, with redemption coming in the form of the birds.

Many of the great Victorian specimen and trophy collectors wrote biographies and bird-oriented travelogues, even before Audubon published *Ornithological Biography* (see pages 46–47). A number of these books made it onto the shelves of public libraries, where later generations of active birders were able to plough hungrily through the works of Guy Mountfort, Jim Clegg, Bruce Campbell, Jim Corbett, Frances Hamerstrom, Richard Meinertzhagen, Allan Moses and others, writing about Britain, the colonies and North America.

Inspiration abounded from such globe-trotting adventures, but with a more home-grown focus, perhaps no book epitomised the genre to greater effect than *Seventy Years of Birdwatching* by H G Alexander (1974). Chronicling the discoveries of a birding career which began in the reign of Queen Victoria and, at the time of completion, was still going strong in the Seventies era of Ted Heath's government (albeit latterly with a more American focus), it captured many a birder's imagination with what could be achieved with a life-long interest in birds.

Subsequently, a new kind of inspiration became apparent when Richard Millington's *A Twitcher's Diary* (1981) appeared on shelves, impressing on go-getting binocular-slingers just what level of listing could be achieved in one year, with spare time and determination

H G Alexander's memoir demonstrated to younger
birders and ornithologists just how rich, full and
productive a life of observing birds could be.

(and perhaps either a private income or hefty
credit). Many such books have come since then,
often highlighting an extreme competitiveness
that can be off-putting from what is often
regarded as the fun sub-hobby of listing.

Birding memoirs and biographies still arrive
annually today, and in quantity. A modern
memoir often begins with a dramatic change in
life, perhaps reflecting the contemporary
writer's more inward-looking stance. Job is
lost, a divorce decreed, an illness diagnosed or
overcome – a new lease of life, a freeing from
some responsibility leads to a reconnection of
the (usually) middle-aged (normally) male

protagonist, with mixed results. Recent such
volumes have tended to anal retention, often
being a listing memoir appealing to a limited
but committed audience – only birders can
travel the world and have little to say about the
culture and avifauna of the countries visited,
just the numbers and species names.

There are exceptions to this, with authors
like American Mark Obmascik, whose enjoyable
The Big Year (2004) was made into a far more
mediocre movie, and Australian Sean Dooley
(*The Big Twitch*, 2005) creating reads that crossed
over to members of the non-birding public by
their literary merit and capacity to entertain.

73 : Asolo Scout shoe

1975

Birds often live in inaccessible and sometimes severe habitats, and to see them in the wild, birders must venture into that inhospitable environment. To do this in comfort or even to survive, they must don appropriately rigorous apparel.

The history of outdoor clothing extends back into times when humans pretty much lived outdoors. 'Ötzi the Iceman', a 5,300-year-old or so preserved man excavated from a glacier in the Austrian alps, had the remains of what is believed to be either a snowshoe or a backpack associated with his corpse. With that kind of history, it is impossible to say when these or any other basic item of outdoor attire was first developed.

Clearly, any item of clothing intended to be resistant to the elements could be termed 'outdoor', but the 20th century saw great innovations in baggage, footwear, insulation and outer wear that would be adopted by, and eventually designed specifically for, birders.

Traditional external frame backpacks have been known and used by both mountaineers and the military for many centuries, but these developed metal frames in the mid-1900s, followed by the internal frame introduced in 1967 by Greg Lowe of Lowepro. The semi-rigid design makes a large pack more comfortable to carry, and a detachable daypack without a frame is also sometimes incorporated into the design. Such packs, waterproof and highly durable, are essential in rainforest and desert expeditions, and with capacities up to 50 litres can fit optics including scope, tripod, clothes and books for trips lasting several weeks.

Outdoor clothes tend to be designed for the extremes of cold, heat or wind or, in the case of footwear, for rugged terrain. Though people have long needed to cross rough substrates and mountaineers were ascending peaks for leisure by 1874, when Europe's highest mountain was conquered, it wasn't until as recently as 1975 that the first specifically designed lightweight hiking shoe, the Asolo Scout, was developed.

Prior to that, by 1920 Adi Dassler and his company – the now ubiquitous Adidas – had developed a running shoe for athletes, and both strands of footwear manufacture were contributed to by orthopaedic medicine when shoes with arch support were first produced. Asolo's lightweight Scout shoe was the logical consequence of this; manufactured from leather and nylon, it was designed for trekking alpine trails. Many other companies have since followed suit, and there is now a crowded

Asolo Scout shoes were the first lightweight shoe specifically designed for hiking, and as such, commercially deposed the market in cheaper but less comfortable surplus armed forces footwear.

market for all styles of walking, hiking and climbing boots and shoes, often with the innovatory Gore-Tex fabric included (see pages 144–145).

Gore-Tex and other layered and chemically impregnated fabrics can also be found in the wide range of coats, trousers and field waistcoats now available. Companies such as Páramo (launched in 1984), Country Innovation (1996) and other outdoor clothing specialists have developed garments specially designed for the situations in which birders and other naturalists find themselves. Camouflage colours, waterproof and insulated inners and outers, and multi-faceted storage pockets are incorporated into almost all possible clothing combinations, until squads of birders can resemble paintballing teams, if not the actual military.

However, there is little doubt that such clothing helps conceal birders from their quarry, and even saves lives in extreme conditions.

74 : *The Atlas of Breeding Birds in Britain and Ireland*

1976

One of the British Trust for Ornithology's greatest achievements has been the collation of many millions of observations of common and regular British bird species over decades, so that a true picture of their distribution, movements and changes in populations can be established.

Key to the ongoing accumulation of this data, and a prime motivator too, was the compilation of *The Atlas of Breeding Birds in Britain and Ireland* (1976) and its follow-ups and spin-offs (now including the up-to-date *Bird Atlas 2007-2011*). Compiled in association with the Irish Wildbird Conservancy (now BirdWatch Ireland), the original mighty tome mapped out the breeding distribution of all the birds of the British Isles, recruiting volunteers from the birding public to census birds at sites using rigid 10-kilometre squares (subdivided into 25 'tetrads' which are 2x2km squares), giving the observations a real scientific rigour and meaning.

The project followed in the wake of the innovatory *Atlas of the Breeding Birds in the West Midlands* by J Lord and D J Munns (1970), the first book to use the technique, as well as Perring and Walter's *Atlas of the British Flora* (1960). Forming an Atlas Working Group in 1967, the BTO was able to draft in almost 15,000 birdwatchers to submit their records over the period 1968-72.

The format of the first Atlas, as it simply became known, used 250 maps, with three dots in decreasing size variously representing the confirmed, probable or possible breeding respectively of all 218 species of British breeding birds. It became an essential purchase for all birders interested in their country's avifauna, as well as an invaluable ornithological and conservation tool.

Logically enough, *The Atlas of Wintering Birds in Britain and Ireland* (Lack 1986) followed a decade later, covering the winters of 1981 to 1984, and the second breeding bird atlas was published in 1994, covering the period 1988-91. This last work used exactly the same methods to enable changes to be compared directly in scientific papers and within the book itself.

Another major variation on the theme was *The Migration Atlas* in 2002, a substantial addition to the literature on the subject, this time using modified techniques to plot bird movements generated through a huge volume of national and international ringing recoveries. The most recent and ambitious atlas project yet develops the formula still further, covering

Up-to-date atlases of bird distribution are essential for birders
wishing to locate their local or nationally scarce birds, and enable
them to contribute their own sightings for the biological record.

both the breeding and wintering distributions
of the national avifauna for the period 2007-
11. Better resourced and with greater support
from birders, it utilised the services of 40,000
'volunteer recorders' to map over 216 million
birds through 182,230 timed tetrad visits, 5.3
million 'roving records' and another 4.5
million records submitted through the BTO's
online BirdTrack scheme.

Such an efficacious format has caught on

worldwide, with similar methods being used in
virtually every county, state, province, region
and country with a bird club, ornithological
society or bird conservation organisation.

Data gathering has only been sharpened by
the online presence of the BTO's BirdTrack
website and its long-running American
counterpart eBird, both of which have ambitiously
expanded beyond their core national areas (see
pages 188–189) to gather data worldwide.

75 : *Big Jake Calls the Waders*

1980

The popularity of Ludwig Koch and Max Nicholson's early forays into commercial wildlife vinyl record releases launched the commercial viability of bird song recordings in particular, though now such recordings tend to be birder-specific rather than bought by the general public. Over time, bird vocalisations have been released on all the major recorded media, with vinyl records, cassettes, 8-track cartridges, compact discs and downloadable MP3s all being available to bird aficionados.

A few key recordings have been influential or notable in the formative history of many birdwatchers. HMV's *Bird Recognition: an Aural Index* series of EPs (1965), recorded by Victor C Lewis, gave many birders a handy reference to the sounds of a lot of our most common birds, while the oil conglomerate Shell, in the guise of Shell Nature Records, put out nine 7-inch EPs covering a fairly comprehensive slice of the British avifauna from 1966 to 1969 in its *British Birds* series. Witherby's *Sound Guide to British Birds* (1969) carried the calls and songs of 200 species on its two 12-inch discs.

For the serious student intent on actually learning bird songs and calls, the only option in the late 1960s and 1970s was the music cassette, largely because a tape could be listened to in the car or at home, and later on a portable cassette player, with or without headphones. Consequently, series like the popular *Teach Yourself Bird Sounds* became a pivotal purchase in many a nascent field birder's career.

At the turn of the 1970s two relatively comprehensive multiple disc series of European bird songs were released: *The Peterson Field Guide to the Bird Songs of Britain and Europe* (1969-1973) was launched as an unwieldy 14-disc reference set, while Jean-Claude Roché's now fairly ubiquitous Western Palearctic recordings were issued on a 15-disc 10-inch set and at least two five-record sets. The quality of Roché's recordings has resulted in them still being available today. Cassette and vinyl sets were released for all the continents around this time, though their quality and comprehensiveness was variable.

Some recordings are remembered by birders for their novelty value. One such disc, here symbolising the genre, was *Big Jake Calls the Waders* (1980), a vinyl LP of wader call imitations by well-known birder Jake Ward, who is still part of the birding scene today. With its protagonist on the cover resplendent in early Seventies' knitted headwear and resembling a minor

HavenAudioguides

BIG JAKE

CALLS
THE WADERS

Commentary: BRYAN BLAND
Produced by : ALAN HAVEN

MILLSTREAM
RECORDS

Like a progressive rock Percy Thrower, 'Big Jake' showed how responses could
be produced from wild birds by impersonating their calls. Nowadays field
birders are more likely to use digital recordings to elicit the same reaction.

progressive rock keyboard player, the record
has plenty of kitsch appeal even now,
though it never claimed to be an essential
educational aid.

Notwithstanding some descriptive errors in
the original accompanying literature, the
2,817 recordings of 819 species in *Bird Songs of
Europe, North Africa and the Middle East* by Andreas
Schulze and Karl-Heinz Dingler (2003) were
the European birder's avian Rosetta Stone early
on in this century, available initially on CD
and then MP3. But the fast-spinning evolution
of digital technology means that even these
masterly recordings have now been overtaken.
The ease with which amateur and professional
field recordings can be uploaded to websites

and blogs has enabled the Xeno-canto website
(www.xeno-canto.org) to completely dominate
the field for birders needing an accurate
collection of bird recordings for almost any
destination on the planet.

This Dutch online archive is an open-
source, searchable collection of the world's
bird calls and songs, and at the time of writing
held 158,598 downloadable recordings of
8,886 species. Soon the site, which is free to
use by both recordists and visitors, may well
hold recordings of virtually every species and
subspecies on the planet. A world away from
Big Jake and his shorebird impressions, it is an
invaluable and irreplaceable resource for
birders and ornithologists everywhere.

76 : Compact disc

1981

Trumpeted on launch as the great new recording medium, CDs enjoyed a long and successful run in the wake of the cassette tape era. Although the party's not yet over, the format is now waning steadily, and ultimately it is destined to go the way of all recording media which preceded it.

Introduced in 1981, it was essentially a miniaturisation of the commercially unsuccessful LaserDisc format developed by Philips, MCA and Pioneer which was used for a short while for movies and videos in the 1980s. Other than as a digital carrier of bird sounds for retail, an alternative use of the CD was as a data storage medium in the form of a CD-ROM.

This purpose was also short-lived, though forward-thinking company BirdGuides had several successful titles such as *The CD-ROM Guide to British Birds*, *The CD-ROM Guide to Rarer British Birds* and *The CD-ROM Guide to All the Birds of Europe*. The retail format was primitive compared to more modern alternatives, but a large amount of graphics, photos and text could be stored, though the data was merely burnt onto the disc by laser and then read rather than edited afterwards.

The straightforward audio CD is still useful as a high-quality playable disc, and continues to be used by the ultra-contemporary team at The Sound Approach, who usefully append two recorded CDs of bird vocalisations with each of their plushly produced books of ruminations and esoteric modern bird lore.

For other publishers, the DVD format has become increasingly popular, storing a far larger volume of data, making the format ideal for movies. DVDs permit scrolling between tracks and cross-referencing, making each species or scene watchable in moments, rather than the time-consuming rewinding and fast-forwarding of tape formats.

Some of the BirdGuides titles have also been available as DVDs – including company founder Dave Gosney's *Finding Birds In ...* series – while Paul Doherty's well-filmed Bird Images video series was also released in DVD format after debuting on VHS tapes. But perhaps the most recent innovation in DVD has been Bob Flood and Ashley Fisher's *Multimedia ID Guide to North Atlantic Seabirds*, a multi-part work first released in 2011 which contains detailed identification text on tricky seabirds in book form, with accompanying DVDs showing original filmed footage on the kind of pelagic trips for which the authors are so well known.

DVDs can also be bought blank like CDs and used for archiving original photos, sound files and documents, though with far greater storage capacity – typically ranging from 4.7-17 GB (gigabytes) for different DVD formats, compared to typically 700 MB (megabytes) for CDs. But though both have been used widely by birders, the advent of cheap computers with serious amounts of on-board storage, external

The CD-ROM Guide to **British Birds** Version 7

2 DISK SET

Covers 330 species
Over 700 video clips
Over 700 illustrations
Nearly 300 photos of nests, eggs and fledglings
Over 500 distribution maps
Over 2000 screens of text

Jean C. Roché
4
All the bird songs of Britain and Europe

Spieldauer 19:20 Stunden | 2.817 Tonaufnahmen | Mit Begleitbuch

Andreas Schulze

Die **VOGELSTIMMEN**
Europas, Nordafrikas und Vorderasiens

819 Vogelarten
17 Audio-CDs

The compact disc has turned out to be a less permanent format than first envisaged, with the advent of DVD and then downloadable sounds, but they are still practical for transferring recordings onto computers.

hard drives and 'cloud' space, where hosting companies provide storage or sharing facilities on privately owned secure servers, has seen the formerly widespread popularity of burnable optical media decline significantly.

Also commonplace now are convenient USB or flash drives, pluggable into any computer and some other devices, often small in format though with reduced storage capacities to match. The choice of media on which to publish or store countless bird photographs, sounds, notes and references has never been wider — the only real issue likely to impact upon their success in the birding community, as elsewhere, is the lack of back-ups and the potential loss of unique material.

77 : IBM PC

1981

Few inventions have had a more comprehensive effect on how we research, record and store information about birds than the personal computer. While PCs in their original form were actually available in the mid-1960s, these were little more than glorified calculators with print-out capabilities. For most people it was only two decades later when desk-top – and later laptop – computers became commercially available that the revolution truly went digital.

Early home machines by Commodore, Apple and Atari, with up to 64 kilobytes (kb) of memory (about the size of a low-resolution thumbnail image today), offered few applications and were not widely adopted for general use. Their potential became apparent among biologists as they developed, but to the hobbyist naturalist, it was IBM's 5150 Personal Computer, unveiled in August 1981, that was the first of the genre. The take-up wasn't immediate on a large scale – at $1,595 a system it was never going to be – but as technology advanced and manufacturing capacity increased, prices came down and personal computers, including Amstrad's UK-marketed alternatives, became far more commonplace.

By the 1990s, installed and 'outboard' hardware like recordable media, coupled later with the widespread availability of the internet, enabled the transfer and storage of large volumes of birding data. Latterly, the amount of memory available in computers, external hardware and online storage sites has become exponentially huge. Birders think nothing now of archiving many thousands of high-resolution images, a library of PDFs and scans of reference books and plates on their home computers, while the advent of broadband and WiFi have made it even easier to compile and share these resources via the web.

Today, such is the progress in mobile technology that photos and observations can be circulated from the field and images uploaded from a phone while the observer is still chest deep in a reedbed. Identification problems can be resolved using references downloaded via the 'cloud' to compare visuals and vocalisations of a given bird species, while birders can post GPS co-ordinates to pinpoint the precise location of any bird or site.

Much of this explosion in digital birding is inextricably entwined with the internet, providing immediacy of access to information over increasingly rapid and mobile connections. Where would birders be without such technology? Most now use a computer for

Few birders are without a PC or laptop these days, and the machines
have taken over all aspects of reporting, documenting, analysing and
discussing birds as our personal hubs of reference and retrieval.

recording their notes and sightings in various
ways, sharing them with friends, local bird
club websites and national organisations, and
storing and editing photographs.

Many also post online to personal blogs,
news services such as BirdGuides.com and
social networking sites, and debate sightings
and other issues of the day on forums. Indeed,
birding news and opinion is now often shaped
by the sometimes brutal democracy of equally
weighted access, and both anonymous and
sourced contributions. The expertise or

accuracy of online contributors is often
swiftly tested in such open courts, and it
usually becomes known quite quickly whose
opinion and 'gen' to trust and who is a fraud,
who is over-frivolous and who can generally be
relied upon.

It is now almost impossible to imagine the
days where binoculars, a notebook and a field
guide were all that was required to enjoy
birding – today, digital technology of some
kind in general, and a computer in particular,
are almost prerequisites.

78 : Sony Handycam

1985

On the windy morning of 1 October 1995, David Ferguson and Jo Wayte were walking on the cliff-top path near Land's End, Cornwall, when they found an unfamiliar warbler flitting around on the ground. Unlike most birders at the time, David Ferguson carried a video camera along with his optics, and he managed to get a few seconds' worth of shaky but identifiable footage of the bird – crucially, including some evidence of the almost site-specific local flora.

His suspicion that it was a Bay-breasted Warbler was borne out by the video, and forensic analysis of the footage tied the plants to the location, thereby confirming the first ever occurrence of the species on the European side of the Atlantic. Without the critical video evidence, such an extreme record would be far less likely to gain acceptance.

Although not widely adopted by birders at the time, camcorders had undergone a general surge in popularity a decade earlier, when Sony launched Video8. An alternative to the compact VHS-derived VHS-C format, Video8 helped revolutionise home movie production in the 1980s in much the same way as Super 8 had done in the 1960s (see pages 138–139). Preceded by Sony's Betamovie – the first

one-piece consumer camcorder – and Betamax and Betacam product lines, Video8 offered state-of-the-art compactness for amateur film-making, with camcorders for the first time small enough to fit in the palm of a hand. This enabled users to shoot movies easily on their own, recording events onto cheap and durable video cassettes. The format also had superior audio quality to most rival formats and longer recording capabilities than VHS-C.

One of the first Video8 camcorders to be successful commercially was the Handycam, introduced by Sony in 1985 and doing for video what the Walkman did for portable music players. Video formats continued to develop rapidly, however, and though Video8 persisted before giving way to the better-quality Hi8 format, it was the larger, longer and better-quality VHS cassettes that became the consumer product of choice after 1987, when full size VHS cameras were introduced to the market. Ultimately, analogue formats quickly waned following the introduction of digital video.

It was the advent of digital camcorders and then video functions on both compact and DSLR cameras that brought the biggest surge

Camcorders soon replaced Super 8 as the film
recordists' machine of choice, but are now themselves
being usurped from popularity by pocket cameras and
DSLRs with expanded video capability.

in video recordings of wild birds, from
backyards to rarities worldwide. And no longer
did shooting footage of birds mean a
significant financial outlay on equipment:
using accessories such as inexpensive iPhone
adapters for telescopes, recording relatively
good sequences became easily achievable with
just a mobile phone and telescope.

While that is welcome progress, video
footage is not necessarily always the last word
in bird identification. Amid much fanfare in
2005, and largely on the basis of blurred video

footage, Cornell Lab of Ornithology
announced the rediscovery in Arkansas, USA,
of Ivory-billed Woodpecker, a highly
charismatic species declared extinct in 1996.
Unfortunately, the announcement proved
premature, the film later being rather
convincingly shown to involve a poorly filmed
Pileated Woodpecker. By this time the
'rediscovery' had not only made headlines
globally, but led to the reallocation of a small
fortune in conservation dollars, as well as spark
a healthy line in woodpecker souvenirs

79 : Kodak Electro-Optic Camera

1987

Birders who made the transition to photographers were relatively few before the turn of the 21st century, but it is now commonplace to see a long lens or digiscoping kit hanging over the shoulder of seemingly every other person at a reserve or twitch.

Digital cameras have been a boon for the birder, whether for mere record shots or for sharp images approaching professional standards. That's not to say the skill, judgment and eye for a picture borne of experience are now unnecessary, but it is easier than ever for even the most casual dabbler in photography to produce serviceable images.

The other real advantage of digital photography is the lack of film. Old-fashioned cameras entailed up-front costs for film and processing, but digital cameras can now store thousands of high-quality images on a single reusable memory card, easily transferable to a computer or hard drive, and storable there or online. Software such as Adobe Photoshop can then be used by the photographer rather than a specialist developing lab to enhance the quality further and in microscopic detail, while in the case of RAW files even the settings used for shooting can be adjusted after the event. If there's a downside, it is that such ready image manipulation creates opportunities for mischief and fraud for the less scrupulous photographer.

Working with digital images may seem second nature these days, but digital cameras have not actually been around for that long. The first attempt to convert electrical signals from light into pixelated images came in 1975 when Steve Sasson, an engineer at Eastman Kodak, developed a charge-couple device (itself originally invented in 1969) for digital imaging – essentially, the first image sensor.

The first DSLR (digital single lens reflex) camera was Kodak's Electro-Optic Camera, designed and built for the US government in 1987, but it was impractical as it came with a huge storage pack. Fuji introduced the DS-1P in 1988 which had a more useful 16 MB internal memory. Shortly after, DSLRs entered the US commercial market in 1991 in the form of the Kodak Professional Digital Camera System (DCS 100 for short).

Strange though it may seem now, digital imaging techniques were initially poorly received. The DCS 100 was cumbersome and not really practical in the field, as it used a digital image sensor in a standard Nikon F3 body connected to a large and heavy shoulder

Kodak's Electro-Optic DSLR had what would now
be considered as a ridiculously small memory,
but its innovations were far-reaching.

pack containing a Digital Storage Unit with a hard disk holding a then-impressive 200MB of data at 1.3 megapixels per image. Originally aimed at sports photographers and photojournalists, at a retail price of up to $30,000 it understandably sold fewer than a thousand units.

But the format continued to develop rapidly, and with increasing popularity came lower costs. Digital compacts caught on more quickly before the price of DSLRs made them truly affordable, but the latter have numerous advantages over their smaller siblings. These include not only the obvious benefit of interchangeable lenses with longer focal lengths, but larger image sensors enabling much better performance in low light, less 'noise' (visible as 'graininess') in the resulting images and much faster autofocus and shutter responses — perfect for fast-moving or flying birds.

It was inevitable that camera manufacturers would look at the middle ground between the two formats, and ultimately the bridge camera was borne. These relatively lightweight models approach the size and range of DSLRs but utilise a small sensor and have a single integral lens, in the case of modern 'superzoom' models often with impressively long-range focal lengths of up to 50x magnification. This is the equivalent of a 24-1200mm lens in 35mm terms, and while the optical compromises necessary for the small 'footprint' of such models mean the results won't be as high in quality as those of comparable DSLR equipment, they are still clear, sharply focused and reasonably true to life.

Importantly, bridge cameras offer a significant cost saving over the combined cost of DSLR camera bodies and lenses, making telephoto photography affordable to an even greater number of birders.

80 : Perkin Elmer Cetus
DNA Thermal Cycler

1987

An apparent bane of the traditional birder's life is the cryptic species, an entity now more prevalent as the process of DNA analysis and the production of phylogenetic trees have become increasingly important in taxonomy and biology.

The discovery of DNA's correct form by Watson and Crick in 1953 and the realisation that each species carries its own unique arrangement of this chemical code could only have confused an ornithological world which relied on physical dissimilarity for its identification of bird forms.

The first fairly comprehensive revision of bird relationships by Sibley and Ahlquist in 1990 used the DNA-DNA hybridisation technique, in which DNA from one species is labelled and compared with another's in the hope of determining how closely related it is. Some of their conclusions are controversial or, like the claimed close relationship between New World vultures and storks, now largely disproved by later refinements, but it was the first and most major in a long line of taxonomic reshuffles which have continued to illuminate relationships between bird species.

The large-scale analysis of small quantities of DNA — for instance, that taken from the toe pads of bird specimens — was made possible by the polymerase chain reaction (PCR) technique. Thermal cycling — heating and cooling in rotation — to produce a polymerase chain reaction was first tried by biotechnology firms in 1983, using an enzyme from a heat-resistant bacterium to 'unzip' DNA into single strands and 'amplify' these exponentially until they can be detected, identified and compared. A formal *in vitro* procedure was invented in 1985, but the first machine was developed by the American laboratory machine suppliers Perkin Elmer in 1987. These machines, despite costing between $5,000 and $10,000, became the standard for biologists and forensic scientists until the end of the 1990s. Now they can be obtained at online auction for around $150, but disputes over the various patents associated with the technique and the enzymes used have continued to this day.

This process is still viable, and enables scientists to produce phylogenetic trees to show interlinking evolutionary relationships and to identify mystery birds like the 'Flamborough flycatcher' in 2012, which was initially thought on plumage to be Britain's first Atlas Flycatcher, but shown in the laboratory to be a straightforward Pied Flycatcher.

Thermal cyclers (top) belong in the lab and not the field, but in the case of cryptic species,
if we really want to know what we are looking at, then sometimes they are essential. Such
technology solved the mystery of the Flamborough Flycatcher (right), initially thought to
be an Atlas Flycatcher (left) but revealed to be a Pied Flycatcher (centre).

81 : British Birdwatching Fair poster
1989

After a two-year gestation period during which it evolved from an event called The Wildfowl Bonanza, the British Birdwatching Fair – or more simply Birdfair – was finally born in 1989. This annual event takes place at the extensive Rutland Water Nature Reserve, Leicestershire, a drinking-water reservoir owned by Anglian Water that opened in 1976, after the former Empingham Reservoir was dammed and extensively reworked.

Co-founder of the event, Tim Appleton, said: "On a personal level, I had been at Rutland Water since 1975 and, though keen to stay on there, I needed new challenges. I went to a nearby game fair (there are several around the country) and it struck me that as the shooters and hunters had such an event, why not birders?" He contacted his friend Martin Davies at the RSPB, and held a meeting in the appropriately named Finch's Arms to discuss how to convince those involved in the already burgeoning birding industry to take part. A big help was Bruce Hansen of binocular retailer In Focus, who contacted the major optics manufacturers, all of whom leapt at the idea. Clothing, travel and publishing companies followed suit.

Rutland seemed ideal, being almost dead centre of 'populated' Britain, with good rail and road access, and plenty of hotel space. This was to prove particularly important as the event grew, with every hotel for up to 50 miles now usually fully booked, often from the previous year.

Initially, the agricultural land surrounding the artificial but wildlife-rich wetland found use as a grassy forum for a small selection of stalls and marquees that in the first year attracted about 3,000 people, raising some £3,000 to help stop hunting in Malta. Attendance has consistently risen to more than 20,000 in recent years, with 11 marquees, two smaller lecture tents and numerous food and drink stands catering for entertainment and refreshment needs.

Taking place annually over three days in August, the full-time staff at Rutland are augmented by scores of volunteers from both the reserve itself and from the RSPB and wildlife trusts – the staff have truly grown with the fair, and the organisers are at pains to point out the essential help of the scores of volunteers, many of whom have returned year after year, only for non-material rewards.

The contributions to conservation have been significant, too – not just financially, but in promoting little known but crucial global, and often cross-border, projects and objectives. Successes include funding the initial campaign against long-line fishing in 2000, helping to prevent the unsustainable number of albatross deaths caused by this poorly targeted tuna-fishing method; David Attenborough's keynote 2008 speech in Peterborough on birds-of-paradise, which attracted more than 1,400

The first-ever Birdwatching Fair in 1989 attracted some big name birders was was a village fête compared to the rock festival-sized affair it has become in recent years.

people; and the discovery on a Birdfair-funded expedition to Burma of more than 5,000 pairs of Gurney's Pitta, a species previously believed to number just dozens.

The event has always avoided UK-centred projects, regarding them as already well-catered for, and instead consistently aimed for a local to national to international flow of funds and publicity, in some ways pre-empting the current vogue for the protection of birds' flyways and summer and winter territories together — a kind of holistic approach to conservation. Birdfair's conservation themes have evolved over the decades from saving particular forests and deltas in developing countries like Vietnam and Ecuador to continental-scale campaigns like the most recent support for BirdLife International's Preventing Extinctions programme, most recently focusing on the migratory flyways of the Americas in the fair's 25th year.

The event is also central in providing a commercial market for the entire birding industry — artists, writers, publishers, optics manufacturers, ecotravel companies and guides, and garden bird food specialists

— enabling bird enthusiasts of all kinds to try out and purchase the latest innovations and products, and to socialise and network in what is also the world's biggest ecotourism fair. It also has great importance in drawing attention to pressing conservation issues, and accordingly each fair has an over-arching theme every year, collectively raising a sum its founders estimate to be more than £3.3 million to date. This is aided by the large number of attendant celebrities freely giving their services, as well as the selfless volunteers.

The marquees attract a substantial number of international participants in addition to British birders, and the success of the Rutland event has seen it echoed in some form on every continent bar Antarctica. In fact, Tim Appleton says that he is perhaps proudest of the number of similar events that have sprung up around the world, like wind-blown seedlings. This has resulted in matched funding with many of the other fairs for projects in their countries, to the tune of more than £20 million and counting — perhaps the UK event's greatest legacy of all.

82 : Microsoft Powerpoint

1990

The nationwide network of local bird clubs and RSPB members' groups provides a small but enthusiastic lecture circuit where acknowledged field experts or local birders back from trips at home or abroad can present their photographs and findings to a sometimes appreciative audience. But those who have suffered the frustrations of a temperamental slide projector, upside-down images or a paper-shuffling, mumbling presenter will be grateful for Microsoft's introduction of Powerpoint as one of its cornerstone software packages.

Powerpoint was originally designed for Apple computers and launched in 1987, but it was soon acquired by Microsoft and relaunched alongside Windows 3.0 in 1990. It was at this point that its revolutionary capabilities to make presentations well illustrated and bullet-pointed became apparent to a wider public. The ability to compose 'slides' containing graphics, photographs and words saved a lot of time for presenters and lecturers, and provided much more well-presented and

succinct content for an audience.

Commonly used by both teachers and students in schools, the program has now widely replaced whiteboards, blackboards, slide projectors and long-winded and convoluted lecture notes in classrooms, as well as for audiences of birding talks. Other advantages are that a presentation's entire content is now easily transportable on a small USB stick and playable on almost any computer, and handouts of talks are easily generated.

Laser pointers are often used in conjunction with Powerpoint, and these tiny and powerful devices also have a controversial use in the field; many bird tour guides have taken to pointing out birds at roost or nest at night or in dark undergrowth or forest with these intense light beams. However, there is a danger of damaging an animal's eyesight with such devices and birds can be frightened away by the beams (hummingbirds are notoriously easily spooked by laser pointing). Used judiciously, laser pointers can be very useful in field birding situations as well as the lecture hall.

Powerpoint is an easy way to illustrate lectures and talks, and many birders use it when presenting their photos and observations to bird clubs and interested gatherings.

83 : First website

1991

There is an argument that, without the internet, a personal computer is little more than a glorified calculator and word processor – it is as a communication device that it really comes into its own, and in this interlinked capacity the machines have revolutionised birding as much as any other special interest.

At its most basic, the internet is a global network of networks – a system which interconnects millions of different private, commercial and governmental computer networks. Its roots stretch back to the early 1960s, when researchers first attempted to synthesise digital messaging formats and rules for the exchange of messages. The first protocols for 'internetworking' were developed by British computer scientist Donald Davies in the early 1970s.

The decommissioning of the ARPANET – the first collaborative 'packet switching' program that connected different computer systems – and consequent removal of commercial restrictions on linking networks enabled near instant communications between users, both individually and en masse.

The real revolution in birding terms has come with the huge amounts of free information and storage available online, enabling use and sharing of data and images from the field and between observers at home and at work. Remote and hands-on access to information is equally possible, and observers can exchange news and comments via social media like forums, blogs and networking sites, and exchange text messages with ease.

The most personal way of reporting sightings and observations has been through the creation of an individual website, though recently the immediacy and convenience of a blog (originally 'web log') has been the presentation method of choice for most. Websites are also data collection points for large-scale citizen science projects such as the RSPB's Big Garden Birdwatch and Cornell Lab of Ornithology's eBird project (see pages 188–189), as well as specialist bird image resources such as the 250,000-plus photos now archived on BirdGuides.com. Importantly, the web has provided online shop-fronts for a wide range of birding

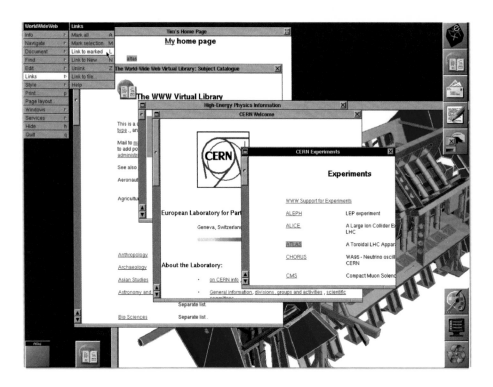

Screenshots of the first website only hint at the internet's now near-universal adaptability and usage, and just over two decades later it is almost impossible to imagine daily life, let alone birding, without it.

businesses including publishers, bird news services, manufacturers, writers, artists and ID gurus, all presenting their solid and abstract wares in a fast, click-smart market-place.

All this has been made possible by the development of the World Wide Web, conceived by Tim Berners-Lee in 1990, and then provided free for all in 1993. It was established to manage information on the already inter-linked computer systems of the internet, neatly bracketing the launch of the first website in 1991.

The ability of individuals to create their own personal, interactive and viewable online space within minutes is one of the many revolutions of the internet, and the full repercussions are probably still some way off being felt.

84 : Rare Bird Alert pager

1991

With telephone-based bird news services becoming well established in the 1980s (see pages 146-147), information on the presence of interesting species, especially rarities, was not hard to come by if you were near a telephone. But what if you weren't? Stories of early twitches where the target bird disappeared long before excited birders arrived on the scene were rife.

That problem was likely to keep recurring as long as the onus was on birders to find out what was about. At peak times in the field, getting up-to-the-minute news could mean dispensing a small fortune in silver into a public payphone, and it was simply impractical as well as expensive to keep phoning premium rate lines just in case something new had turned up near you. Clearly, in the days when mobile phone ownership was very much still a luxury, there was a real need for a more efficient means of communicating the whereabouts of sought-after rarities.

Although it took time for the birding world to realise it, the required technology actually already existed. Pagers had evolved as a parallel branch of mobile telecommunications and had been widely used in the commercial and public service sectors for some years. First patented by

Al Gross in 1949 and initially used by medical staff in The Jewish Hospital, New York City, USA, by 1959 many emergency services were using pagers that received short-range radio signals. The first commercially available pager was introduced by Motorola in 1974, and by 1980 there were 3.2 million users of these early limited-range devices, which became long range a decade later. At the technology's peak of popularity, there were 61 million pager users worldwide in 1994.

Pagers tend to operate as a subscription-only service, with the provider offering a series of options from which users choose their favoured combinations or packages. An individual pager is assigned a unique phone number, usually shorter than mobile or landline numbers, and this receives either messages to call an answering service to collect voice messages or actual texts containing the desired information. The pager unit most frequently beeps to alert the user of an incoming message, and these beeps can vary according to the level of urgency or importance of a message or, like a modern mobile phone, can also vibrate or give out pieces of programmed music. The messages are usually transmitted via satellite.

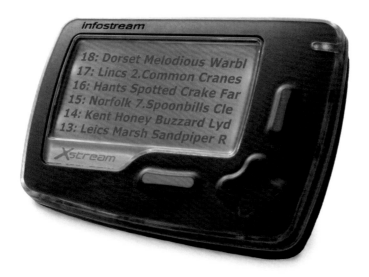

Initially used mostly by doctors and hospital staff, the immediacy of pager alerts and the comparatively reasonable price of the technology easily lent itself to the world of birding, in particular those who sought rarer birds.

The potential for revolutionising the delivery of rare bird news at a realistic cost was something that Norwich-based birder Dick Filby recognised first. In 1991 he launched Rare Bird Alert (RBA), a dedicated bird news pager system which was quickly embraced by the active twitching community. The pager became a must-have birding accessory for some, and the concept attracted other start-ups such as Birdnet and Birdcall. Although the former, in particular, attracted a following, RBA was comfortably the pager market leader and remained well ahead of the pack. The quality of the service has also become more refined over the years, with users able to select regions of the country and level of rarity as part of their service.

With regularly updated sightings information transmitted direct to users, pagers are still one of the most efficient ways of getting up-to-the-minute news. Pager 'black spots' with little or no signal are less of an issue now even in the more out-of-way locations, and two-way pager communication technology is within sight, offering new possibilities.

At the same time, there is no doubt that text messaging services, Twitter, the mobile internet and dedicated smartphone apps have broadened the bird news market and opened up new – and often cheaper – technological routes to solving the same problem that pagers so effectively dealt with in the past.

85 : *Birdwatch* magazine

1992

Though ornithological journals had been widely published since the 19th century, as the hobby of birding became more popular to the layman, a need developed for more accessible magazines than even the less academic journals like *British Birds* (see pages 96–97).

Bird conservation organisations had their membership titles, of course – for example National Audubon's *Audubon Magazine* (founded 1899) and the RSPB's *Birds* (launched in 1903 as *Bird Notes and News* and latterly retitled *Nature's Home*). But in the post-war period, a populist birding press was needed to cater for the growing numbers of those whose own expertise and experience was outflanking the field guides, but for whom scientific journals were too dry and detailed.

Monthly magazines would be the ideal medium for carrying the latest advances in field birding, ornithology and identification, but it took some time for any to emerge. In the US the American Birding Association's *Birding* was first published in 1969, following a year as a kind of mimeographed fanzine called *The Birdwatcher's Digest*; the latter title was launched as a popular monthly magazine in its own right by the Ohio-based Thompson family in 1987.

Back in Europe, the bilingual *Dutch Birding* took off in 1979 as a less staid continental counterpart to *British Birds*. It was followed in the mid-Eighties by two British launches, the generalist *Bird Watching* (1986) from commercial magazine publisher EMAP, and the hardcore *Twitching* (1987) from the team behind the Birdline news service. The latter title was renamed *Birding World* a year later, but as the decade came to a close the middle ground in ornithological publishing remained empty.

Catering for more serious news issues, identification problems and the growing trend towards global birding, in 1992 a new independent magazine, *Birdwatch*, was launched. EMAP's response was to introduce the quarterly *Birds Illustrated* as a second 'spoiler' title to its stable at the same time, but it was less of a success and, after several lavishly produced issues, the plug was pulled. After *Birdwatch*'s first year as a bi-monthly, subscription-only title, it became monthly, took on staff and went on sale nationally in the newsstands.

Firmly anchored between existing periodicals and catering for an eager audience, *Birdwatch* remains the monthly mainstream magazine of choice for serious birders and has covered a huge range of stories, from exclusives on first British records such as Red-billed

BIRDWATCH
Volume 1 Number 1 £2.15   MAGAZINE   January/February 1992

Is there hope
for the Barn Owl?
AMERICAN
WARBLERS
IN THE UK
Rarity highlights
from 1991
World birding
Bird photography
Win a pair of
Leica 10x25s

COLLECTOR'S ISSUE

The first issue of *Birdwatch* wasn't available in the shops, but
signalled the advent of real birders' expertise into the mass
market-place when it went nationwide a year later.

Tropicbird to the unprecedented confession of the fraudster who conned the national rarities committee into accepting a fabricated record of a Hermit Thrush in Essex (at the time, supposedly just the fifth for Britain).

While their history is in print, all the world's birding magazines see their future at least partly online, and some — notably *Birdwatch* — are embracing social media and other channels. Many industry commentators continue to see a future for niche printed magazines, but only time will tell whether digital editions will take the lead from the traditional paper and ink versions.

86 : Gitzo Mountaineer carbon fibre tripod

1994

Camera tripods are essential to stabilise photographic equipment and were rapidly adapted from supports for astronomical telescopes, evolving into specialised birdwatching telescope stabilisers during the late 20th century.

Much of the early history of tripod use for telescopes and cameras is lost, though they were used for surveyors' theodolites in the 19th century, and ornate carved tripod supports for early astronomical telescopes are known from the 17th century at least.

The vast majority of photographic and scope tripods use a design with a central height-adjustable column through the junction of three collapsible telescopic legs that are lockable in typically three sections (sometimes two or four), either using clips or screw-grips to lock the legs in place. The head is normally a detachable column-mounted unit with a screw-threaded mount plate, in turn also detachable, and a handle or adjuster to help the user control the angles in which the head tilts, pans and rotates. Bags or weights may be hung from the base of the central column to further stabilise the unit. Heads can be ball or pan-tilt, the former using a ball and socket joint, the latter with different controls in varied lockable planes, allowing a smoother pan and precise anchoring in position.

Reasonable quality tripods were often constructed from aluminium until the 1990s, when the advent of carbon fibre enabled strength, stability and lightness to be possible in one unit, a weight-reducing boon for use in the field. Gitzo's Mountaineer model, launched in 1994, was the world's first carbon fibre tripod. While photography is the main market for the company, along with other firms such as Manfrotto, Slik and Velbon, tripods specifically aimed at birders' telescope requirements are now also widely produced.

Though used by a very small minority, monopods – one-legged supports with simpler head designs – are gaining in popularity, due to the ease with which they can be set up and collapsed, as well as their lightness. Some units can even double as a walking stick.

Another very recent innovation in tripod design has been the Gorillapod, manufactured by San Franciscan company Joby. A small unit for cameras that uses three flexible legs to wrap around branches and fences, the Gorillapod enables a camera to be stabilised in most habitats where a full size tripod might not fit. The device is modelled on the grip of great apes, hence its name, and is composed of linked chains of nine ball and socket joints.

Tripods were quickly adapted from the world of photography to support and transport telescopes, and this was hugely aided by the development of carbon fibre models for lightness combined with strength and stability. A Gitzo tripod being used to photograph a Snowy Owl in Canada is shown here (top), while the adaptability of the innovative Gorillapod is put to good use in rocky terrain (above).

87 : MP3 file

1994

Perhaps the most convenient method of transferring aural information devised so far has been the MP3 file, which despite the reservations of hi-fi and music buffs is undeniably a very practical format with which to record and play bird calls and songs.

Though in production for some years previously as part of MPEG moving image files, MP3s were first used as separate entities under that name in 1994, their use spreading rapidly on the internet and really picking up as part of the audio player Winamp, which enabled users to encode, create and exchange their own files.

MP3s encode digital sound data using 'lossy compression', a way of making data more compact and storable by losing extraneous parts of the source. This relies on a phenomenon called auditory masking, in which the presence or effect of a sound is cancelled out by other frequencies. It is the same phenomenon that was recently discovered to cause the songs of urban songbirds to have their lower frequencies masked by the noise produced by human activities, resulting in lower breeding success in city centres.

Sound sources can be stored without loss as .wav files or other proprietary file types, but they are much larger so take up significantly more storage space, and are therefore less portable. To create an MP3 file, compression algorithms are used to eliminate non-essential sound information. Rather a lot of wavelength and tonal information can be lost before the human ear registers lessening quality, and this is particularly true of the relatively small amount of information contained in most bird sounds – changes to their songs do not appear to be noticed by birds during playback, either, although this has been contested.

Editing software can also be used to crop MP3-encoded sounds to their essence, erasing unneeded elements, and this can be performed on a PC or even on a phone with a sound-editing app.

With the smaller file sizes resulting from compression and trimmed files, far more recordings can be stored in a smartphone, MP3 player or other device capable of playback, and can be carried easily in the field. MP3 players and iPods are small and lightweight and can hold many gigabytes of data, larger models having enough potential space for multiple recordings of every bird call and song in the world (even though this would be unnecessary for most practical birding purposes).

While bird calls and whistles are effective in the field, some birders use
MP3s played on their phones or iPods to attract birds into the open; the
more 'analog' method is also still popular in the USA.

Recordings can also be backed up and
downloaded in the field from the 'cloud' or
from specialist websites like Xeno-canto.org.
Whether for foreign trips or local birding,
bird sounds can then be learned in virtually
any environment, or used to help identify
sounds heard or recorded in the field. Sound
waves from such recordings can also be
rendered as sonograms (pages 130–131) for
analysis and comparison with others.

The polar opposite of such high-faluting
technology is the bird call or bird whistle,
traditional bird sound imitators of which many
have been developed, from simple carved
wooden models to modern metal and plastic
objects. Particularly popular in Scandinavia
and North America, whistles and calls (in this
sense, calls are the actual whistles themselves)
were mostly developed for hunters of ducks and
gamebirds, but many exist now to imitate the
likes of Skylark, Blackbird, pigeons, Common
Cuckoo and numerous American songbirds.
These simple metal and plastic serrated discs
are now available for birds from all continents.

Some birders even have a gift for imitating
bird calls and, though not everyone can call
the waders like Big Jake (see pages 160–161),
many can summon up a decent 'pish' or squeak
with practice, and attract warblers, tits and
crests by making high-pitched and sibilant
noises. In the MP3 age, however, such skills are
surely on the wane.

88 : Open Diary blog

1994

Blogging has such a ubiquitous presence online today that it is easy to forget just how recently this method of keeping a journal and maintaining a website appeared in both birding and wider circles.

Essentially, a blog – derived from 'weblog' – differs from a website in that it features discrete posts published in order of date and time. It can be open to public scrutiny, sometimes with visitor comments on posts, or private, and viewable only by subscription or invitation. Generally, a single person keeps the blog, but multi-person blogs were introduced in 2009, and in birding circles this has been particularly successful in the case of 10000 birds.com.

What we now know as a blog originated in Usenet or Bulletin Board forums, and more specifically from a Massachusetts Institute of Technology (MIT) Media Lab page called Open Diary, maintained by Claudio Pinhanez for a couple of years from November 1994. A different Open Diary was probably the first social networking software, launching in 1998, but by the end of that year there were still only 23 known weblogs on the internet. A year later there were tens of thousands, the difference being the launch of Pyra Lab's www.blogger.com. The huge boost in popularity of what had hitherto been a quite parochial and personal form saw Blogger acquired by Google within four years.

With explosive growth triggered by 'push-button publishing', as Blogger described it, birders quickly adopted the technology. Today there are countless thousands of professional and amateur birding blogs covering every conceivable aspect of the hobby, from general birding and tour diaries to more specialist topics such as ringing studies or taxonomy. A significant number also routinely feature other quirky subjects, from pies to indie music, in an effort to make them stand out from the growing crowd. A blog can be specific to a single trip or patch, or reflect the birding life and philosophy of its writer; it can belong to a birding company or to a known birding 'guru', and accordingly attract a legion of followers.

A rapid development in 2005 was the brief and immediate stream of consciousness form of so-called tumblelogs, which soon developed into the now-essential (for many) microblog. Though Twitter has created a worldwide phenomenon through the facility to say something quickly – and globally – within 140 characters, other sites like Tumblr.com

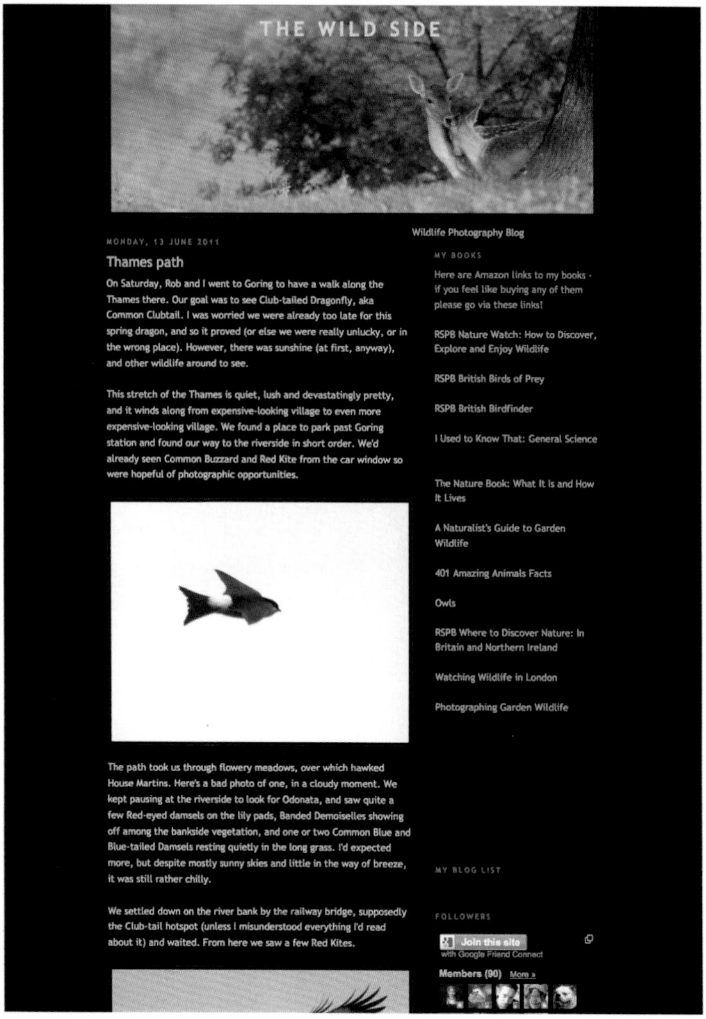
THE WILD SIDE
MONDAY, 13 JUNE 2011
Thames path
On Saturday, Rob and I went to Goring to have a walk along the Thames there. Our goal was to see Club-tailed Dragonfly, aka Common Clubtail. I was worried we were already too late for this spring dragon, and so it proved (or else we were really unlucky, or in the wrong place). However, there was sunshine (at first, anyway), and other wildlife around to see.
This stretch of the Thames is quiet, lush and devastatingly pretty, and it winds along from expensive-looking village to even more expensive-looking village. We found a place to park past Goring station and found our way to the riverside in short order. We'd already seen Common Buzzard and Red Kite from the car window so were hopeful of photographic opportunities.
The path took us through flowery meadows, over which hawked House Martins. Here's a bad photo of one, in a cloudy moment. We kept pausing at the riverside to look for Odonata, and saw quite a few Red-eyed damsels on the lily pads, Banded Demoiselles showing off among the bankside vegetation, and one or two Common Blue and Blue-tailed Damsels resting quietly in the long grass. I'd expected more, but despite mostly sunny skies and little in the way of breeze, it was still rather chilly.
We settled down on the river bank by the railway bridge, supposedly the Club-tail hotspot (unless I misunderstood everything I'd read about it) and waited. From here we saw a few Red Kites.
Wildlife Photography Blog
MY BOOKS
Here are Amazon links to my books - if you feel like buying any of them please go via these links!
RSPB Nature Watch: How to Discover, Explore and Enjoy Wildlife
RSPB British Birds of Prey
RSPB British Birdfinder
I Used to Know That: General Science
The Nature Book: What It Is and How It Lives
A Naturalist's Guide to Garden Wildlife
401 Amazing Animals Facts
Owls
RSPB Where to Discover Nature: In Britain and Northern Ireland
Watching Wildlife in London
Photographing Garden Wildlife
MY BLOG LIST
FOLLOWERS
Join this site
with Google Friend Connect
Members (90) More »

While field observations often disappear into a drawer forever when kept in diary or notebook form, the advent of online weblogs or 'blogs' has enabled birders to share their sightings, opinions and observations with other like minds all over the globe.

and the status updates of Facebook and other social networking sites have also revolutionised the way people interact with each other, including birders quick to capitalise on these new media.

These free-to-join networks are now widely used to disseminate innermost thoughts, trivia and observations, and are also ideal for spreading the news of bird sightings and birding products, both between individuals and between companies and their customers. All such services can trace their history back to that early MIT 'diary' which unwittingly shaped the future of the online world.

89 : eBird

2002

The tracking of the seasonal and long-term changes in bird populations started properly with the institution of bird atlas surveys by the British Trust for Ornithology (see pages 158–159) and the rapid spread of this idea across the conservation and global landscape. However, such endeavours take a lot of manual data managing – it would surely be better if data could be entered by the observers themselves, and a computer could take care of its compilation, analysis and even its partial interpretation.

This idea was quick to take hold among ornithologists and conservationists, and the best, most forward-thinking and globally comprehensive application of the concept is eBird. Launched by the Cornell Lab of Ornithology in New York, USA, in 2002, eBird is an online database of user-generated bird sightings designed to show the actual – as opposed to estimated – state of bird distribution, numbers and abundance to biologists and amateur birders alike. Originally restricted to Europe and North America, its remit was stretched to include the entire globe by June 2010.

It is perhaps a crowning achievement of 'citizen science', the concept of ordinary members of society making their observations of nature count as part of a communal retrieval system of data. The concerns of birders – notoriously obsessed with rarer species – being pernickety about correct identifications and accuracy of counts are addressed through a system of expert data reviewers. But in any case, the advantage of such huge accumulations of data as eBird is that incorrect or inaccurate observations can be lost in the whole, becoming statistically redundant in the overall general accuracy of the 'big picture' figures and trends.

Almost simultaneously with the development of eBird in North America, between 2002 and 2004 the BTO itself was running a public observation survey called Migration Watch. This project was able to record the arrival times of British summer visitors, as well as their geographical spread and concentrations, on a virtually daily basis. To gain a more complete picture, the organisation began to extend the project to record departure times and then the presence and reach of every bird species throughout the year.

This extension mutated rapidly into BirdTrack, which to this day remains the single most comprehensive record bank of British

With its easy to use and user-friendly features, eBird
looks very much like the future for online bird recording
and is now becoming inter-continental in use.

bird sightings. Observations from other websites such as BirdGuides.com and those submitted from the field via mobile apps are also fed directly into the BTO's system. Crucially, rather than operating as parallel but stand-alone schemes, an historic agreement in April 2013 saw eBird and BirdTrack enter into a data-sharing coalition, a special arrangement that will bring huge benefits.

Already the assembled data give a scientifically interpretable account of the impact of climate trends as they happen, and as the broader patterns emerge over the project's long-term existence, the effects of these changes can be observed and perhaps even mitigated to an extent. Data from eBird and

BirdTrack, along with other more specific sources, already shows that half of the world's bird species appear to be nesting earlier than before, a state tightly correlated with climatic and meteorological data from the same time periods.

With the development of such programming capable of handling huge amounts of data, the contributions of citizen scientists are now transferred from their notebooks to part of a purposeful whole. In theory, we all realise we have a small part to play in noting the changes in the world around us, and that these very observations could help save the birds we watch, and the wilder countryside we enjoy while seeing them, for future generations.

90 : Nikon Coolpix 4500

2002

Combining a digital compact camera with a telescope to take images of birds, or more concisely 'digiscoping', began to take off at the turn of the millennium, after the late Laurence Poh developed the technique and took to posting the results on his blog. The method in essence uses the telescope as a surrogate zoom or telephoto lens for the camera, resulting in far greater magnification than the largest prime telephoto lenses.

Using a camera with an optic had been around long before this, though more obscurely. In 1962, for example, Swarovksi Optik launched the 8x30 and 10x30 Habicht Monoculars, using a half porro-prism device which screwed onto the lens of many typical pocket cameras of the time. The same company's AT80 HD telescope, released in 1991, came with an adapter that could be fitted in place of the eyepiece to allow the attachment of a film camera, producing an equivalent focal length of about 1100mm, though with a slow aperture.

But it was the consumer availability of digital compact cameras that helped popularise the technique, which was long known by astronomers with their fixed telescopes and long exposures. Most birders already had

spotting scopes, so the addition of nothing more than an inexpensive compact camera and a cheap adapter to achieve telephoto photography made perfect sense – and in this respect, digiscoping was birder-led practice rather than manufacturer-designed technology.

Of the wave of new compact cameras that followed the advent of digital photography, one stood out above the rest. The Nikon Coolpix 4500 was introduced in May 2002, and for some time after was the digiscoper's camera of choice. A swivel-lens model, it featured a then sizeable 4 MP sensor, had a 4x optical zoom lens and many manual controls; the 1.5 inch rear LCD now appears tiny by today's standards. Crucially, though, the Coolpix 4500 could be easily fitted to the eyepiece of a telescope by utilising the camera's lens thread to attach a purpose-machined adapter. Not infrequently, imaginative birders intent on their own solutions instead contrived ingenious home-made couplings from washers, bottle tops, rubber bands, melamine chopping boards and pieces of scrap wood and metal.

It was actually the 4500's predecessors that first caught Laurence Poh's eye. In February 1999 he started taking photos with the Nikon Coolpix 950 and 990 and a Leica APO-Televid

With its distinctive split-body swivel design and small lens, Nikon's
Coolpix 4500 compact camera became an unplanned successs in the
emerging market for digiscoping equipment soon after the Millennium.

77mm spotting scope, and quickly began
blogging his results using a free Angelfire
website. Tracking the development of his
technique on his website until his death in
September 2004 is effectively to keep abreast
of all relevant developments. The attempt to
obtain sharper images led to the use of a cable
release in conjunction with a custom-
manufactured brass mount, with the scope on a
base plate to avoid the whole assembly tipping
off-balance. Most universal adapters have
simply refined these self-built solutions.

Poh found the Coolpix 4500 to be
incompatible with his set-up, but the model
became popular due to its small lens which
minimised vignetting (that is, the blurring or
darkening of the edges of an image, a frequent
artefact of shooting though a telescope), the

split-body swivel design enabling the screen to
be viewed from different angles, improved
resolution and affordability.

Digiscoping has since increased in
popularity worldwide, and as well as third-
party adapters most major optics
manufacturers have produced adapters for
their own equipment. These range from the
expensively engineered Swarovski DCB II
swing design to Kowa's simple but remarkably
effective plastic iPhone adapter.

Some birders have moved on to DSLR
photography (see pages 168–169) and others
have embraced the improving format of digital
bridge cameras, but it seems likely that
digiscoping, with its simple yet effective
combination of telescope and compact camera,
will have a place for some time to come.

91 : *The Migration Atlas*

2002

Where do birds go? It's a question which has perplexed Man for millennia, long before the concept of migration was understood. While bird movements were widely observed and occasionally remarked upon in early literature, myths prevailed and a few remained popular even as recently as the 19th century. Swallows, for example, were sometimes believed to hibernate at the bottom of lakes, doubtless because of their habit of roosting in reedbeds in large numbers in autumn before suddenly vanishing. A published account from the same era purported to describe three living but dormant Corncrakes excavated from a dung heap in Monaghan, Ireland.

The dispelling of such fanciful beliefs required hard evidence, something which finally became possible with the advent of ringing (see pages 82–83). Ringing has remained the essential method of directly monitoring the movements of birds for more than a century since, but with a recovery rate of no more than 0.18 per cent at its highest, huge numbers of birds must be caught and ringed for meaningful knowledge to develop.

Early migration studies can attribute their success to a tradition of catching migrant songbirds for the pot. On the German North Sea island of Heligoland, migrant thrushes were trapped for food using *troosel-goards*, or 'thrush bushes' – spaces about six metres long by two metres wide, surrounded by a wall of bushes placed close enough together to let the birds only enter at the bottom, with a net over the top and another on the ground itself; birds were then scared to the centre of the bushes, becoming entangled in the net.

This ingenious method was adapted for bird ringing as the Heligoland trap in 1919 or 1920 by Dr Hugo Weigold, using a more funnel-like arrangement leading to a walled wooden trap at one end. The first British Heligoland trap was erected on Skokholm, Pembrokeshire, in 1933, and this means of trapping has since been used to great effect by bird observatories and migration hot-spots from Shetland to Scilly. More portable options later came in the form of fine-gauge nylon mist nets, no heavier than a mosquito net, and ideal for use in the field. In time, the volume of trapped birds, and thus ringing recoveries, grew to a substantial level.

Ultimately, however, the immense amounts of data collected over more than a century had to be fully analysed to draw useful conclusions about the movements and changes in migrant bird populations. Countless scientific papers have derived from ringing activities, but the greatest mainstream summary of knowledge is *The Migration Atlas*, published by the British Trust for Ornithology through T & AD Poyser in 2002 from the vast amounts of information collected since ringing started in 1909.

Data from more than half a million recoveries of 188 bird species in Britain and

Surveys being undertaken using a mist net (above left) and Heligoland trap (above centre). The wealth of information on birds' international and global movements provided by ringing recoveries has been an ongoing revelation, and the most important and interesting discoveries were documented in *The Migration Atlas*.

Ireland were set out in full and a further 73 species ringed in smaller number were featured in shorter accounts. The maps in the hefty but engrossing tome were the focal point for many birders, visualising epic journeys and feats of nature determined only through those decades of ringing study: Welsh Manx Shearwaters reaching south-east Brazil; a Stone-curlew ringed in southern England and recovered in Mallorca; Arctic Terns in southernmost Africa; even migrant Blackbird, Ring Ouzel, Redwing and Song Thrush on Heligoland. *The Migration Atlas* illuminated such movements for scientist and birder alike in unprecedented detail, demonstrating the value of the practice of ringing.

More than a century after ringing commenced, it clearly remains an important tool in our understanding of the movements of migrant birds. But innovative micro-tracking and tagging techniques are now filling in the gaps with real time continuous movement data (see pages 152–153), again partly due to the persistence and curiosity of the BTO.

92 : *BWPi*

2004

The advent of the DVD format – originally short for digital video disk and first introduced in 1995 – represented a major step up from CD (see pages 162–163). Capable of storing far more data, one DVD could be used to record a then impressive 4.7 gigabytes in a single layer, or up to 8.5 GB with dual-layer recording. With its improved playback of moving images, higher-quality sound and better durability, it was the ideal format to replace video tape for commercial films.

Many birding videos previously released on VHS got a second lease of life on pre-recorded DVDs, known as DVD-ROMs because data could be read only and not written or erased. This included some of the titles produced by BirdGuides – including company co-founder Dave Gosney's *Finding Birds In …* series – while Paul Doherty's well-filmed Bird Images videos were also re-released as DVD-ROMs. The improved format's interactive features also enabled much scrolling between files and cross-referencing, making each species or scene watchable in moments, rather than the time-consuming rewinding and fast-forwarding of standard video cassettes.

The pinnacle of DVD-ROM use in birding came with the 2004 publication by BirdGuides

of *The Birds of the Western Palearctic* interactive, or *BWPi*. The digital version of the benchmark Oxford University Press handbook which was originally published in nine volumes over 17 years from 1977 to 1994, it was a remarkable achievement. The book itself was extraordinary enough, covering 970 species and featuring detailed text, maps and colour plates for all of those regularly recorded in the region. In its DVD reincarnation, however, the entire content of 7,045 pages was now condensed into a single disc just 12cm in diameter.

Oxford University Press had itself previously attempted to issue the magnum opus as a DVD-ROM, but the publication had been beset with technical problems. *BWPi*, too, had a few glitches, but the availability of such an easily searchable detailed and expansive summary of all the region's birds more than made up for these difficulties. Version 2.0 followed just two years later, but the difficulties of keeping such a key reference updated using optical media mean that further revisions were cancelled.

Like the CDs that preceded them, DVDs were also sold as blank recordable discs and saw much use for the back-up and transfer of birders' own photos and documents, though subsequently they have lost out to inexpensive

BWPi brought encyclopaedic knowledge of the
Western Palearctic's avifauna to birders' fingertips,
and the updated format may still prove useful despite
the accessibility of online information.

external hard drives which are far more
capacious for storage and much more practical.
Cloud back-up and web file-sharing services,
some of them free, have further compromised
the latter-day appeal of DVDs, as have
miniature but large-capacity portable
USB memory sticks.

None of this stops data from being
corrupted, however, and the biggest memory
costs the largest amount of money for a tiny
device that can be easily lost. Still, the choice

of media on which to store many thousands of
photographs, sounds, notes and references has
never been wider, and a routine of regular
back-ups should eliminate the need to worry
about the long-term survival of precious data.

It seems likely that with the recent
introduction of field guides as both ebooks and
smartphone apps, the days of the DVD-ROM
medium are numbered, but it has proved a
good way of storing and retrieving masses of
information in an accessible format.

93 : Kowa Prominar ED TD-1 Spotting Scope and Digital Camera

2004

With the explosive boom in the birder-driven phenomenon of digiscoping in the early 'Noughties' (see pages 190–191), it was clearly likely that manufacturers would respond to demand by trying to answer an obvious question: 'Why not just incorporate a camera into a telescope?' In 2004, Kowa did just that with the TD-1.

Stylish in its day, relatively portable at 2.3kg and compact at 39cm in length, the model temporarily looked set to revolutionise the taking of bird and wildlife photographs. The unit operated both as a straightforward scope for observation and, with the flip of a switch, a digital camera with a powerful 10-30x zoom lens – equivalent to 450-1350mm in 35mm format terms.

However, once released and field tested its weaknesses became apparent. It was limited by a low 200 ISO rating, restricting use to good lighting conditions, and the aperture of f2.8 at 10x became f4 at 30x. Though an issue with many digital cameras of the day, there was noticeable shutter lag. Autofocus had an alarming tendency to drain the power out of the four AA batteries, and though mains power could be used when connected to a PC for image transfer, the AC adapter cost extra (as

did other accessories). Bizarrely, the paltry 32 MB SD card provided with the TD-1 was, according to the instruction manual, the largest size permitted for use, despite much larger SD cards being available at the time. Perhaps worst of all, however, was that the focus reset itself after each shot, meaning that critical fast-fire sequences were impossible as the user had to continually refocus the TD-1 on the target bird.

These drawbacks limited the appeal of an otherwise innovative product. More fundamentally, there was a major inherent problem with this kind of hybrid device. At 3.1 MP the TD-1's sensor was already notably undersized at release date, when many cameras boasted much bigger sensors. Technology progresses fast, but sensors are integrated components which cannot be updated, and while upgrading to a better camera might cost hundreds of pounds, upgrading a telescope is a much more expensive (and therefore rare) affair: the TD-1 retailed at a hefty £1,760 on launch in 2004, representing no small investment, and depreciation was likely to be heavy.

Effectively from the outset of production, these shortcomings meant that its days were

The TD-1 was an innovation almost immediately overtaken by other developments, but the basic idea may still see more long-lasting fruition with further technological advancements.

numbered. Kowa's TD-1 proved a relatively brief phenomenon, with manufacture ceasing by 2009 and no successor models launched. Other companies have experimented with products in the same area, including photo eyepieces for telescopes from Zeiss and Minox, and Zeiss's impressive but expensive PhotoScope 85 T*FL – selling at a colossal £4,785 suggested retail price in 2011.

Birders, the key market for such products, are so far unconvinced by the claimed virtues of camera-telescope hybrids. Perhaps one day brave optics companies will find a way to overcome the significant design, performance and upgrading issues, but in the meantime advances in DSLR, bridge and compact cameras, not to mention digiscoping accessories, have made their job tougher.

94 : Scopac tripod backpack

2005

A largely unsung hero of birding is that humble foot soldier of the gravel path and muddy track, the pedestrian birder. He or she doggedly heads for inaccessible reserve or non-infrastructured estuary using only public transport and boot leather, often carrying telescope, tripod, camera and bins through rain, snow or sunshine. For that sturdy individual, the backpack tripod carrier has been a godsend.

Succeeding where previous carry-strap attempts failed, the Scopac, and its close cousins the Mulepack and the discontinued Viking Tripod S'port, enable a birder on foot to carry a telescope still attached to its tripod on his or her back, leaving both hands free for using binoculars or taking photographs. This is made possible simply by attaching two of the tripod legs to what is essentially a small flat triangular backpack. The tripod can still be opened, and can even remain partially extended, while the built-in straps and adjusters spread the weight of the load in such a way that the scope and tripod feel much lighter than if carried over the shoulder. Cleverly, the design means that the equipment and carrier do not need to be separated from each other whenever the wearer stops for a scan.

Features vary according to model but typically include one or more pockets for a field guide, notebook or small camera, while the 'Lite' version of the Scopac offers a separate detachable Digipac storage pouch with water bottle pocket. A further advantage of this particular model is the use of breathable mesh material; as well as cutting down on heat retention and sweating, it helped negate the 'sail effect' of designs using solid canvas, which could be caught by strong winds and blown over if left unattended while attached to a standing tripod.

As a side benefit of this novel and popular invention, the birding backpack also means that more are encouraged not to use their cars to help transport their gear; it is also entirely suitable for birding excursions by bike, sealing its green credentials.

Though ignored by many more mobile birders, telescope-bearing backpacks like the Scopac have proved a boon for pedestrian birders, or those who use public transport or bicycles.

95 : Rainham RSPB visitor centre

2006

There have always been nature reserves of a sort since humans gathered into tribes or nations, whether they were designated hunting or fishing territories for a king or priest, or taboo areas in which such practices were expressly forbidden.

The first state-sanctioned reserve is generally taken to be the Drachenfels in northern Germany, a mountain which was protected from quarrying, its previous use, by the Prussian government in 1836. Yellowstone National Park in the USA was the first reserve as we would understand it, being preserved from human settlement and exploitation in 1872, but in Russia Il'menskii, a *zapovednik* ('sacred area', to be kept forever wild), was the first site to be protected primarily for the study of nature in 1919.

The securing and promotion of Britain's 2,000 or more nature reserves demanded facilities for visitors. Local authorities, wildlife trusts (originally by created by Lord Rothschild in 1912), the RSPB and other bodies have been intermittently installing visitor centres on their sites since the beginning of the 20th century, though some have been very basic indeed and other locations still have no facilities, even after decades of

use. The importance of having amenities for the public became more apparent in the 1960s and 1970s, when the RSPB stepped up its land acquisition programme after predicting the squeeze on bird-rich habitats for decades. A wave of visitor centre construction took place from that period onwards.

The new era of state-of-the-art, environmentally friendly visitor centres is best typified by the somewhat futuristic building at Rainham Marshes RSPB reserve, where industrialised east London peters out into Essex's Thames corridor. Long recognised as a birding hot-spot, the reserve was acquired by the RSPB in 2000 from the Ministry of Defence, which had used it principally as a test firing range, and it was officially opened to the public six years later.

The £2.3 million visitor centre at Rainham is a bold design, its twin-funnelled, multi-coloured façade cloaking a structure which sits on 19 metre-deep pilings in the ground to prevent the River Thames from undermining the building. It boasts green power generation and conservation from photovoltaic cells, passive solar heating, a small wind turbine, a ground heat source pump, sheeps' wool insulation, rainwater harvesting and low

Set against the Thames Estuary landscape, the RSPB's visitor centre at its Rainham Marshes reserve is undeniably striking, to the point where it initially divided opinion among public and conservationists regarding both its cost and its design.

energy lighting. The building won six awards for its sustainable design, including a Regeneration and Renewal Award and a Royal Institute of British Architects National Award.

Since then, other impressive facilities have opened at reserves such as the RSPB's Titchwell, Saltholme and Minsmere sites, and the Norfolk Wildlife Trust's Cley Marshes reserve. The balance between providing ease of access and comfort for the public and the cost of such installations has been precarious, but over time these landmark projects undeniably become a focal point for local communities and help establish such sites on the wider map.

96 : iPhone

2007

While some mobile phones have featured cameras since at least the early Nineties, and the first photos were shared between users in June 1997, it was the development of smartphones that really made the technology commonplace. But taking and sharing photos is just one of many useful capabilities the devices offer, and none offers more to birders than Apple's increasingly ubiquitous iPhone.

There is no absolute distinction between a smartphone and a regular mobile or 'feature phone' other than a general advancement in technological features, but a smartphone can be described as a high-end phone featuring a camera (often with geotagging via GPS), along with portable sound, video and other media players, internet browser, touchscreen and, crucially, the option of thousands of apps – essentially, downloadable mini-programs or information storage and retrieval systems.

Originally co-opted by game producers and retail organisations and now widely used in all fields, apps have helped turn smartphones into pocket personal computers, enabling users to maintain their social networking, emailing, diaries and even the ability to work on the move. Typically, a number of key apps are preloaded on most smartphones, while others can be downloaded according to the user's specific needs. Their popularity means that more smartphone owners now use apps than browse the internet on their devices.

Birding organisations and businesses were initially slow to take up the app baton, but many specialist apps are now available for bird identification and vocalisations, recording observations and trip information, and submitting sightings and receiving news. Some are free, others are paid for. Apple currently has the widest app selection, accessible through iTunes, but Android options through Google Play are on the increase.

Apps for birders can be functional, educational or recreational. In the first category, for example, birders in the field in Britain can report rarity sightings using the BirdGuides app or submit field data to the BTO using the BirdTrack app, just as their American counterparts can using the BirdLog app for eBird (see pages 188–189).

American birders are particularly well catered for with field guide apps. *The Sibley Guide* is available in its entirety as an app, while *Peterson Birds of North America* for iPhone has not only plates and sound recordings, but also articles and even the facility to keep your own list of North American birds. Regional bird sound apps are becoming popular, with the likes of Birdsounds.nl releasing different versions of the same product – such as a full paid-for app featuring 764 species from Costa Rica or a free 'lite' version with 70 species.

iPhone birders can, of course, import their own collection of bird sound CDs via iTunes.

The iPhone leads the way in birding apps, with affordable versions of field guides now entering the market as well as sightings logging, trip reports, general bird information and bird sounds apps, some of which are free.

Playback of recordings is possible using the phone's own speaker or by connecting a more powerful external speaker via the headphone socket. The phone's voice recorder can also be used very successfully in the field to record and play back bird songs and calls, and even edit them on the fly.

And with the camera capable of taking still images or shooting video – with an adapter for 'phonescoping' if required – the combination of built-in features and apps makes the iPhone a veritable Swiss army knife for birders.

Tablet computers have also been the recipients of numerous apps since their full inception from 2002 onwards. While less suited to use in the field, the larger screen size of Apple's iPad models and their Android and Windows counterparts makes the format more suited to apps such as magazine digital editions, which often feature video or sound files to enhance pages from the print edition. Tablets are also better for the new generation of birding ebooks, and Christopher Helm is leading the way in the latter area with the release of enhanced digital editions of its best-selling field guides. Not only do these feature voice recordings for many species, but in theory at least it will now be possible for a field guide to be continually updated with new species, splits and lumps.

97 : Biotope hide

2012

The hide, or blind to birders in North America, is familiar to anyone who has visited a nature reserve. Like many things in birding, it can trace its history back to hunting.

Screens which exist today on reserves as standalone wooden walls with viewing slots placed at eye height, generally intended to obscure the observer from waterbirds, originated prehistorically as somewhat lower walls of interwoven osier or willow stems, or other constructible vegetation, behind which the hunter would hide himself.

More or less the same concealment techniques have been used for centuries since, in more recent times to greater effect as new ways have been developed to improve success. For example, often having 'seeded' the nearby water with decoy ducks, and often using a duck call to imitate the quarry and lure waterfowl to the nearby water, the hunter would sit silently waiting a close approach with his gun (or bow or spear even further back in time).

In North America, strict rules apply to the construction of hunting blinds, with structures not being allowed more than 12 feet above the waterline, but no lower than four feet. These structures must be removed by 1 April, at the end of each season.

Hunting hides tended to be smaller affairs than the pine bungalows used by birders which are found today on many reserves. Usually just big enough for one or two people, a hunting hide would generally be placed on the edge of clearing known to be attractive to deer. A pre-dawn vigil would often result in the hoofed mammals grazing or wandering close enough for a clear shot.

The static hides of the modern bird reserve are typically more elaborate affairs, ranging from garden shed-like boxes with crude bench seats to carpeted cricket pavilion-sized barracks, and to multi-tiered tower hides with 360° views. The three-storey Peacock Tower Hide at the Wildlife and Wetland Trust's showcase London Wetland Centre reserve even has a wheelchair-accessible lift. Many more popular reserves, or those closer to urban centres, have hides that more closely resemble a classroom or lecture theatre, while the RSPB has started to install tall glass walls or windows in some.

Portable hides have generally fallen out of use after moderate popularity in the early to mid-20th century, though photographers still utilise them, particularly when their subjects are lekking gamebirds or waders, raptors that have been lured to a baited area, or songbirds coming to a drinking pool. Cloth hides resembling square tents can be used by birders and photographers to watch ground-dwelling and nesting species, and were popular in India with tiger hunters.

Despite the long history of hides, they are not without their innovators and visionaries.

The bird hides designed by Norwegian innovators
Biotope are masterpieces of minimalist design that
actually work for observers in the field, set up in
open form while still sheltering those inside from
the wind and conserving heat.

Most of the reserves in Britain, whether owned by the RSPB, WWT, Wildlife Trusts, National Trust or private companies or individuals, have at one time or another featured hides made by Gilleard Brothers Ltd, a company that has virtually monopolised hide construction since 1975, when it built its first birding-specific hide at Blacktoft Sands RSPB Reserve. Gilleard's structures are typically plain wooden buildings tailored for different sites, and featuring oblong viewing windows with a wide field of view, along with seating benches and shelves to lean on. This no-nonsense approach has made the company's products affordable, popular and familiar to almost all birders in Britain, but the company has branched into ever-more complex and modern designs in recent years, maintaining its edge.

Newer on the scene are the Norwegian architects and birders Biotope, with a futuristic approach to hides that, in 2012, produced radical new open-sided birding shelters around Varangerfjord. The concept was essentially to rethink the whole 'box with holes' approach to traditional hide design, enabling birders to move around freely inside a modern structure to change their angle of view, while still not disturbing wildlife and being protected from the wind. Also in Varanger, the company Arntzen Arctic Adventures has provided a floating photo hide on a boat, as well as its more standard camouflaged photo hides with gas fires. Such innovative approaches to hide design and function look set to help change the ways in which we view birds at close range in future.

98 : Swarovski ATX
modular telescope

2012

While a substantial part of the history of birding has involved the co-opting of technology ostensibly developed for other purposes, the last few decades in particular have seen the hobby grow its own lucrative demographic, with manufacturers developing and refining products designed specifically for birding needs.

Perhaps the most compensatory for business has been the innovations in the optics industry, with equipment enhancements like lens coatings, nitrogen-filling and weight reduction all being designed with at least one eye on the birding market.

Many of these modifications have been created to solve climatic or transport problems encountered in the field. The crowning achievement in this arena thus far saw Swarovski Optik produce a new breed of telescope specifically designed to overcome the logistical problems of the travelling birder.

Unveiled to the birding media in the wide-open landscapes of the Great Hungarian Plain, the benefits of the ATX series were immediately clear. Its main USP was modularity, the body being comprised of an angled eyepiece module and one of three objective sections – 65mm, 85mm or 95mm.

For the first time a telescope used the same component principles long established in camera systems, with interchangeability of the business end of the optics a major technological breakthrough.

This was coupled with a fundamental change to the design of the eyepiece, which became a fixed, flat-surfaced lens, facilitating rapid adaptability for digiscoping. Unlike with other scopes, a camera and adaptor could now be fitted without interruption for refocusing or adjusting the zoom. Emphasising intention in this respect, a new swing-design digiscoping adaptor also became available at the same time.

The zoom function traditionally performed on the eyepiece was transferred to a ring at the other end of the eyepiece module, where the eyepiece and objective sections locked together. This meant that zooming and focusing could be performed more efficiently on adjacent rings in the centre of the telescope's body, while refinements in the optical elements themselves meant that a clear image could be viewed right up to 70x magnification through the largest objective version (up to 60x on the other two versions).

With its greater magnification and über-light-gathering power, the 95mm is well suited

Swarovski is constantly raising the bar for high-end
optics, and the company's modular scope idea was
acclaimed for its distinctly portable design.

to seawatching and other long-range viewing situations, whereas the less weighty 85mm is better for more mobile general birding. At the smallest and lightest end of the scale, the compact 65mm is ideal for travelling, easily fitting into more capacious jacket pockets once dismantled. The high price tag notwithstanding, Swarovski doubtless hopes that users will opt for at least two objective options to go with the single eyepiece module.

The release of the ATX series was greeted with much acclaim, and was followed in early 2013 by the introduction of its straight-bodied counterpart, the STX series. This optical modularity is mix 'n' match birding at its best, with the only restriction on getting soundly equipped for any field circumstances being your credit limit. Birders will keenly await the response of other manufacturers to this reinvention of the telescope.

99 : *Goldfinches on a wall of pound shop plastic* by Richard Crawford

2012

From many of the objects featured so far, it can be seen that birding as a hobby has been refined by technological developments into becoming a multi-disciplined pastime, often both intellectual and compulsive, and the technology keeps on coming.

But aside from its practical manifestations, birding has also gained a wider presence in the media and arts, particularly in the last two decades. Artists like Richard Crawford notably use urban waste and plastic bought from 'pound shops' as perches for models of common birds, in an attempt to highlight the avian presence in our lives and cities.

Several artists employ stuffed birds in installations and friezes. The most remarkable of these artists is the sculptor Polly Morgan, a trained taxidermist who assembles still life displays of birds and mammals she has preserved. These are collected as roadkill or donated by pet and cagebird owners, and carefully — sometimes disturbingly — placed among man-made materials and objects. The representation of birds, like all art, has come a long way since the Renaissance.

In broadcast media, several documentaries highlighting the more eccentric aspects of twitching have been broadcast on the major

terrestrial channels in both Britain and North America, but the hobby itself has probably been seen as less esoteric over the years, bearing in mind the viewing public's appreciation of a plethora of high-quality wildlife documentaries — when nature looks so intriguing, dramatic and exciting, why would it be quirky or weird to want to see it at close quarters?

It has been claimed that a number of celebrities enjoy birding, and while novelists like Margaret Atwood and Jonathan Franzen are well known for their direct involvement, claims that Mick Jagger and Darryl Hannah are birders are exaggerated at best. However, several pop musicians certainly are. Indie bands Elbow and British Sea Power feature birders among their number, while whole albums by artists such as Piney Gir and Shearwater have featured birding as an inspirational concept.

While the days when birders were widely viewed with suspicion are still with us and glamour is in limited supply, many people from mainstream walks of life seem happy to admit their love for birds and involvement in what can be seen as quite a nerdy hobby; sometimes they even feel able to express that

Richard Crawford's posing of model birds on cheap
plastic consumer goods both highlights the presence of
birds around our commercial endeavours and perhaps
comments on the destructive results of consumerism.

involvement through their art.

Birds are alluring and deeply involving,
being both obvious enough to attract human
attention and secretive enough to give an
observer a lifetime's worth of discovery and
study. Our technology can reveal new layers to
this discovery and our creativity express how we
feel about the innate mystery of unknowable fellow
creatures, but we will never peel back the last layer.

Perhaps that is why a select group of people
return to birds as if they were unfinished
personal business, time after time, never
getting to the heart of their fascination but
always loving its pursuit.

100 : Crystal ball

Even a cursory glance back through the objects in this book will give the impression that the technology of birding has produced an ever-faster rate of invention and innovation. Looking into this last object, our hypothetical crystal ball, there is no reason to think that this will stop soon.

Further evolution of nanotechnology, already so important in bird migration studies, will lead to ever-tinier transmitters — for example, the storage of data within man-made DNA molecules is now possible. The application of graphene-based technology is also in its infancy, and a layer of graphite just one atom thick can be used as a flexible, wearable, virtually invisible and weightless sheet, potentially revolutionising the dimensions, frequencies and power usage of devices including radio and satellite tags.

Radio frequency identification tags are already small enough to be attached to bees, with 2mm aerial-bearing chips now available; the weight and inconvenience of these to a bird is negligible. The Global System for Mobile Communication has potential to track birds and communicate directly with mobile phones, relaying co-ordinates and climatic and directional information direct to project teams; it could even enable experimental manipulation of the subject itself.

Video cameras are now small enough to attach to birds, and continuing miniaturisation will herald an expansion in their use. Dramatic examples of back-mounted video footage have been televised in BBC TV's *Earthflight*, but the novelty belies the scientific applications. Small cameras have already been used to record previously unknown tool-use in New Caledonian Crow.

Owners of iPhones and Android mobiles are enjoying an increasing range of gadgets for their devices' ever-more sophisticated built-in cameras, including digiscoping adaptors and zoom lenses. With each new model, handset technology continues to develop, and with increasing capacity for apps, data storage and software, could it eventually be possible for a smartphone to replace optics, camera, notebook, field guide, sound recorder, bird news service and even an expert human guide?

This last possibility is not as far-fetched as it sounds. Mobile internet use is set to be revolutionised by Google Glass technology, allowing the wearer of web-enabled spectacles to record images and access the internet — shape and colour recognition programs could become available to compare live image feeds with stored information on bird species and confirm identification. It's not a huge leap of imagination from music recognition software such as Spooky and Shazam, the likes of which could also be developed to recognise bird songs and calls while listening 'live'.

Bird identification may also be

Google's new Glass technology may make the wearer think they are looking through the eyes of Predator, but the light, wearable, hands-free head gear opens up a world of mobile possibilities that is only just becoming apparent.

revolutionised in other ways. Portable DNA testers are now available to identify genetic specimens in the field. Tablet computer-sized biosensor devices have been developed to identify infectious diseases like Ash Dieback and H5N1 within 30 minutes, while the Minion is the size of a large USB memory stick, holds a DNA specimen for sequencing and can be plugged into a laptop for analysis.

Future developments in birding extend beyond the technical to the commercial. In conservation, the Worldwide Fund for Nature (WWF) launched the very first conservation mobile network at the end of January 2013 — WWF Wildlife Mobile gives 10 per cent of net call revenues to conservation, which is ideal for the growing number of people with an interest in, or a concern for, the environment.

Conservation charity credit cards have long been marketed by the RSPB and others, but financial business models may be applied and perhaps we will be buying many of our daily consumable products from suppliers that are actually front-end distributors for charities.

What of birders themselves? The threat of environmental catastrophe predicted by scientists has created acute awareness of the problems facing birds globally. Anticipated extinctions are a driver to see — and try to save — vanishing species such as the Spoon-billed Sandpiper while there is still the chance.

At the other end of the scale, there are those outside the worlds of listing and environmental activism who simply thrive on the more aesthetic enjoyment of their local birds. Whether it takes the form of feeding garden birds or systematically recording the species of a local patch, the importance of this cannot be underestimated. If the huge and growing numbers of households taking part in the RSPB's annual Big Garden Birdwatch is a fair indicator, this trend looks set to continue. It is also possible to imagine a reaction against the array of technology into analog birding, where expertise and skill are measured and respected by their ability to find and identify birds all by themselves, old school style. You know — what used to be called 'birdwatching'.

Index

Index entries in **bold**
refer to objects

A

Abernethy Forest RSPB
  reserve 81
Adamson, Lydia 124
Adidas 156
aeroplane ticket 100–101
Afghan Snowfinch 69
Age of Exploration 21, 46, 50
albatross 172
Alden, Charles 148
Aldrovandi, Ulisse 21
Alexander, Christopher 98
Alexander, H G 98, 154, 155
Alexander, Wilfred 98
Allen, Clile 87
alpha taxonomy 26
American Acclimatization Society
  (AAS) 84
American Birding Association
  (ABA)
American Ornithologists' Union
  (AOU) 60, 73
ancient Egypt 14–17, 48, 132
Andersson, Carl-Ove 128
answering machine 92–93,
  102, 147
Antwerp Zoo 48
Appleton, Tim 172, 173
apps 131, 195, 202–203
***Archaeopteryx* specimen 62–63**
Arctic Tern 40, 193
Ardea bennuides 15
Ardea goliath 15
Aristotle 18–19, 20, 22, 44, 52
Arnhemland rock painting
  12–13
ARPANET 176

art 12–17, 22–23, 35, 36–37
  see also avian illustrators
Ashmolean Museum, Oxford 39
Asolo Scout shoe 156–157
Atlas Flycatcher 170, 171
The Atlas of Breeding Birds in
  ***Britain and Ireland* 158–159**
The Atlas of Wintering Birds in Britain
  and Ireland 158
Attenborough, David 110, 111,
  172
Atwood, Margaret 207
auditory masking 184
Audubon, John James 46–47,
  82, 154
The Auk (journal) 60, 112
auks 29
avian illustrators 36, 42, 46–47,
  54–55
aviaries 48–49
aviculture 18, 24, 80, 106–107
Avium praecipuarum (William
  Turner) 20
Avocet 29, 80
Axell, Bert 83
Azure-winged Magpie 63

B

backpacks 156, 198–199
Baikal Teal 128
Bailey, Florence 60
Baird, John Logie 110
Baker, J A 124
Bali Starling 49
banding *see* bird ringing
Bar-tailed Godwit 153
Barbary Falcon 17
Barlow, Peter 86
Barn Owl 37, 117
Barrington, Daines 34
Bartsch, Paul 82
Bay-breasted Warbler 166
BBC Natural History Unit 111
Bell, Alexander Graham 102

Belon, Pierre 20
Bennu 15
Berliner, Emile 66
Berners-Lee, Tim 177
Bewick, Thomas 36, 37
Bewick's Swan 36
Big Garden Birdwatch 80, 176,
  211
Big Jake Calls the Waders
  160–161
binoculars 88–89, 126, 137,
  150
biographies and memoirs 47, 117,
  146, 154–155
Biotope 205
Biotope hide 204–205
'bird flu' 152
bird identification 13, 26–27,
  56, 164, 211
  see also field guides
Bird Information Service 147
bird news services 92–93,
  102–103, 120–121, 146–147,
  178–179
bird ringing 46, 82–83, 98, 152,
  192, 193
bird ringing pliers 83
bird sound recording 66–67,
  76–79, 137, 160–162, 184–185,
  203
bird sound, study and
  interpretation of 130–131
bird table 58–59
bird-nesting pot 24–25
BirdGuides 102, 162, 176, 189,
  194, 202
birding tourism 100–101,
  134–135, 142
Birdland (film) 71
BirdLife International 81, 107,
  173
Birdline 102, 146–147
The Birds of America (John James
  Audubon) 46–47

Picture credits

13 R. 'Ben' Gunn / Margaret Katherine, Jawoyn Elder, 15 Werner Forman/UIG via Getty Images, 17 Detail from E.2.1922: © The Fitzwilliam Museum, Cambridge, 19 Jastrow/Ludovici Collection, 21 Popperfoto/Getty Images, 23 Madonna of the Goldfinch, c.1506 (oil on panel), Raphael (Raffaello Sanzio of Urbino) (1483-1520) / Galleria degli Uffizi, Florence, Italy / The Bridgeman Art Library, 25 Museum of London, 27 Wikipedia Commons, 29 Wikipedia Commons, 31 Horniman Museum and Gardens, 33 Wikipedia Commons, 35 Epics/ Getty Images, 37 Wikipedia Commons, 39 Mary Evans / Natural History Museum, 41t Archive. org, 41b Dietmar Nill/Minden Pictures/FLPA, 43l OpenLibrary.org, 43r Paul Sawer/FLPA, 45t Wikipedia Commons, 45l Wikipedia Commons, 45r Edal Anton Lefterov/Wikipedia Commons, 47l Set of 19th Century Paint Brushes Collection Jim Linderman, 47r Roseate Spoonbill, *Platalea leucorodia*, from 'The Birds of America', 1836 (colour litho), Audubon, John James (1785-1851) / Christie's Images / Photo © Christie's Images / The Bridgeman Art Library, 49 Ben Gilbert, 51b Wikipedia Commons, 51t ImageBroker/Imagebroker/FLPA, 53 Anne Harrap, 55 Mary Evans / Natural History Museum, 57 Bill Morton, 59 Shutterstock/ Jerome Whittingham, 61 LeHigh University, 63 H. Raab Wikipedia Commons, 65 Wikipedia Commons, 67t Olli Niemitalo/Wikipedia Commons, 67b Getty Images, 69 Natural History Museum, London, 71 James Clark Maxwell Foundation, Edinburgh, 73 National Audobon Society, 75 Getty Images, 77 David Hosking/FLPA, 79 Getty Images, 81 Michael Szebor/RSPB, 83l Wikipedia Commons, 83r Mike Powles/FLPA, 85, 87 Museum of the History of Science, 89 Stanislas Perrin/ Wikipedia Commons, 91 David Hosking/FLPA, 93t Valdermar Poulsen/Wikipedia Commons, 93b Carsten Reisinger/Shutterstock, 95l Wikipedia Commons, 95r Getty Images, 97 J. Martin Collinson, 99 Map taken from p.325 of article 'On a Plan of Mapping Migratory Birds in their Nesting Areas' by C J and H G Alexander, *British Birds*, 1909,

101 Don Woodford, 103 Shutterstock/Geoffrey Keith Booth, 105 Ronald Thompson/FLPA, 107l T S Zylva/FLPA, 107r Shutterstock/Atila Jandi, 109t Nigel Redman, 109c Shutterstock/ Stephen Finn, 111 Shutterstock/Stanislav Tiplyashin, 113 Smithsonion Institution, 115l Eric Hosking © David Hosking/FLPA, 115r Houghton Mifflin, 117l Wikipedia Commons, 117r Eric Hosking © David Hosking/ FLPA, 119t Chris Sherlock, 119b Eric Hosking © David Hosking/FLPA, 121 SuperStock, 125 Transworld, 129t J Martin Collinson, 129l Tony Fox, 129r Shutterstock/Nicola Destefano, 131 (sonograms) Paul Morton/The Sound Approach, 131l Neil Bowman/FLPA, 131r Harry Fiolet/FN/Minden/FLPA, 133l Getty Images, 133r Dominic Mitchell, 135 Tiger Tops, 137 David Morton/Recording History, 139 Shutterstock/Daboost, 141 Michael Szebor/RSPB, 143 Nigel Redman, 145 © 2014 W.L. Gore & Associates. This copyright material is reproduced with the permission of W.L. Gore & Associates, 147l Nigel Redman, 147r Bill Morton, 149t Eric Risberg/AP/Press Association Images, 149b Shutterstock/Tororo Reaction, 151t Shutterstock/Eduard Kyslynskyy, 151b Petzl, 153 inset Biotrack, 153 Dean Bricknell (rspb-images.com), 155 Bloomsbury, 159l The West Midlands Bird Club, 159r Bloomsbury, 159b Bloomsbury, 161 Haven Audioguides, 163l Birdguides, 163r Birdsong / Dominic Mitchell, 163b Ample Edition / Dominic M, 165 SSPL via Getty Images, 167 Science and Society/Superstock, 169 James McGarvey, 171t J Martin Collinson, 171l Neil Bowman/ FLPA, 171c Tony Hamblin/FLPA, 171r Simon Spavin, 173 John Cox/Tim Appleton, 175t Mark Sisson, 175b Nigel Redman, 177 CERN, 179 Rare Bird Alert, 181 Birdwatch, 183t Robert Berdan, 183b Joby, 185l Shutterstock/RaidenV, 187 Marianne Taylor, 189 eBird, 191 Dominic Mitchell, 193l Dr Julien Paren, 193r Bloomsbury, 195 Birdguides, 197 Dominic Mitchell, 199 Scopac, 201l Shutterstock/Erni, 201r Dominic Mitchell, 203 Helm/Birdguides/ Sibley, 205 Biotope, 207 Swarovski, 209 Richard Crawford, 211 AFP/Getty Images.

Bibliography

This is a list of the principal references, though many more online references together with private and corporate sources and correspondence were also used in the compilation of this book.

Alonso, P D, Milner, A C, Ketcham, R A, Cookson, M J and Rowe, T B. 2004. The avian nature of the brain and inner ear of *Archaeopteryx*. *Nature* 430: 666-669.

Bircham, P. 2007. *A History of Ornithology*. Collins, London.

BirdGuides. 2006. *BWPi*. BirdGuides, London.

Chansigaud, V. 2009. *The History of Ornithology*. New Holland, London.

Cheke, A, and Hume, J. 2008. *Lost Land of the Dodo*. T & AD Poyser, London.

Cohen, S. 2008. *Animals as Disguised Symbols in Renaissance Art*. Brill, Leiden.

Diamond, J M. 1966. Zoological classification system of a primitive people. *Science* 151: 1102-1104.

Dyke, G, and Kaiser, G. 2011. *Living Dinosaurs: the Evolutionary History of Modern Birds*. Wiley-Blackwell, Chichester.

Ehrlich, P R, Dobkin, D S, and Wheye, D. 1988. *Plume Trade*. http://www.stanford.edu/group/stanfordbirds/text/essays/Plume_Trade.html

Friedmann, H. 1946. *The symbolic goldfinch: its history and significance in European devotional art*. Pantheon Books, Washington.

Grant, P R, and Grant, B R. 2008. *How and Why Species Multiply: The Radiation of Darwin's Finches*. Princeton University Press, New Jersey.

Harrop, A J H, Collinson, J M, and Melling, T. 2012. What the eye doesn't see: the prevalence of fraud in ornithology. *British Birds* 105: 236-257.

Hume, J P, and Walters, M. 2012. *Extinct Birds*. T & A D Poyser, London.

MacLean, I M D, Hassall, M, Boar, R, and Nasirwa, O. 2003. Effects of habitat degradation on avian guilds in East African papyrus *Cyperus papyrus* swamps. *Bird Conservation International* 13: 283-297.

Mayor, A. 2000. *The First Fossil Hunters*. Princeton University Press, New Jersey.

Miles, J. 1998. *Pharoah's Birds*. Printshop of the American University in Cairo Press.

Mithen, S J. 1988. Looking and Learning: Upper Palaeolithic Art and Information Gathering. *World Archaeology* 19: 297-327.

Preuss, N O. 2001. Hans Christian Cornelius Mortensen: aspects of his life and of the history of bird ringing. *Ardea* 89 (special issue): 1-6.

Raby, P. 2002. *Alfred Russel Wallace: A Life*. Pimlico, London.

Rasmussen, P C, and Collar, N J. 1999. Major specimen fra ud in the Forest Owlet *Heteroglaux* (*Athene* auct.) *blewitti*. *Ibis* 141: 11-21.

Schnier, J. 1952. The symbolic bird in medieval and renaissance art. *American Imago* 9: 89-117.

Wade, A D, Ikram, S, Conlogue, G, Beckett, R, Nelson, A N, Colten, R, Lawson, B, and Tampieri, D. 2012. Foodstuff placement in ibis mummies and the role of viscera in embalming. *Journal of Archaeological Science* 39: 1642-1647.

Wallace, I. 2004. *Beguiled by Birds*. Christopher Helm, London.

Winston, J E. 1999. *Describing Species*. Columbia University Press, New York.

www.australiangeographic.com.au/journal/worlds-oldest-rock-art-found.htm; accessed 01.08.12.

http://naturalhistoryofselborne.com; accessed 06.07.13.

www.britishbirds.co.uk; accessed on many occasions.

www.practicalairsoft.co.uk/cwp/notebook.html; accessed 26.08.12.

Biographies

DAVID CALLAHAN lives in east London. He grew up nursing a fondness for birds which saw him toting binoculars on holidays and trips from a young age, as well as pounding his local patches on a regular basis. He has sought avian delights across North America, Europe, the Middle East, Africa and Australia, and trained as a taxonomist at the Natural History Museum. He has been staff writer at *Birdwatch* magazine for six years, as well as contributing pieces to various online blogs and journals.

DOMINIC MITCHELL has been watching birds for more than 40 years, travelling to all seven continents in the process. He is the founder and managing editor of *Birdwatch* magazine and runs the leading bird information website BirdGuides. His previous books include *A Photographic Handbook of the Rare Birds of Britain and Europe* and *Where to Watch Birds in the London Area*. When not studying and photographing gulls on the city's rubbish tips, he is probably away birding in Norfolk, the Azores or the tropics.

Birdwatch

Subscribe from just £9.99*

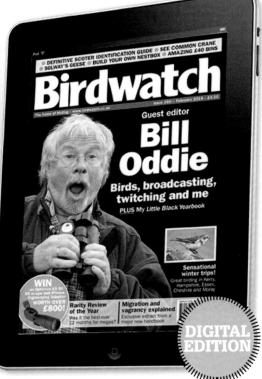

- The UK's number one magazine for keen birders
- Read the latest rarity reports, ID features and much more each month

- Subscriptions start from just £9.99* per quarter (UK direct debit)
- Also available on your digital device from **www.pocketmags. com/birdwatch**

To subscribe visit **www.birdwatch.co.uk** for all the latest offers, or call our hotline on 01778 392027 (quoting 100OB)

*Price correct as of January 2014